Contents

Introduction

Functional skills in Information Technology and Communication (ICT) are directed at encouraging learners to transfer their ITC skills to the solution of real-life problems. As such, this book is not so much concerned with the practical skills of students but whether they can use their practical skills to solve problems using ICT.

Functional skills are available at:

- Entry Level 1
- Entry Level 2
- Entry Level 3
- Level 1
- Level 2

This book is concerned only with the two highest levels – level 1 and level 2. The practical and problem-solving skills for level 2 tasks are roughly at GCSE standard.

Functional skills assess three skills areas:

- using ICT systems
- finding and selecting information
- developing, presenting and communicating information.

> Differences between level 1 and level 2 tasks

In general the differences between level 1 and level 2 are in the complexity of the problems set and the level of technical skills required of the students. However, both at level 1 and 2 the emphasis in functional skills is on independently planning an approach to solving a problem, choosing appropriate software for solving the problem and organising their work in a way that is sensible and logical. Students studying for level 2 are expected to have more practical skills than those studying for level 1. For instance, students taking a level 2 paper may be required to use absolute referencing in spreadsheets, whereas students at level 1 are not required to know about absolute referencing. Students at level 1 are given straightforward tasks that contain a reasonable amount of guidance, but they are expected to demonstrate confidence on making informed selections within that guidance. For instance, at level 1, students are expected to correctly select and open an appropriate application to complete a given task, following instructions. At level 2 the student is expected to plan a solution to a complex task, analyse the stages necessary to solve the given problem independently and to produce a solution and successful outcome using the most efficient methods available.

Further guidance, support materials and sample assessments can be found at the OCR website www.ocr.org.uk.

Students will need access to the OCR ICT Functional Skills website at www.hodderplus.co.uk/ocrictfunctionalskills.

> Structure of this book

This book is divided into twelve chapters. Chapters 1–11 relate to different topic areas found within the Skills Standards and around which tasks might be set in an OCR ICT Functional Skills Examination. Chapter 12 is an examination hints and general summing up chapter and is not associated with any particular tasks.

The format of the examination paper can be found by downloading the Sample Assessment Materials (SAMs) from the OCR website.

Each chapter begins with a formal introduction to the topic and a 'best practice' guide to the skill that is being covered. Following this are a number of tasks based on various scenarios. Most of these depend on files that can be downloaded from the website associated with this book at www.hodderplus.co.uk/ocrictfunctionalskills – each task has a folder of files. Each task is also associated with a Teacher's folder that contains answers, worked examples and a suggested mark scheme.

The website also has worksheets and 'how to' files. There are also some extra chapters containing work which has not been included in the written book, covering such topics as adjusting system settings, protection of computers using anti-virus software and others. It is possible that short written answers may be required in an examination and examples of the type of questions that might be expected are included within these online chapters.

It is not intended that all the tasks in this book are examination tasks. Indeed many of them do not require the independence necessary to solve examination type tasks. Most of the tasks included in this book are intended to be guides as to how a problem could be solved, to act as examples of good practice, and to give the students ideas for future problem solving as well as being fun to undertake. For examination practice OCR has provided Sample Assessment Materials and further guidance on its website. Where an end of chapter task is considered to require the same level of independent problem solving as an examination task it will be indicated by the words **examination task example** at the beginning of the task. It should be noted, however, that OCR may evolve the style of examination papers over time and reference should always be made to recent past papers from OCR for the most up-to-date format.

> Data files

All data files are provided as .doc files as is the practice by OCR for the examination tasks. Students will need to decide for themselves which application to use to solve a task and will need to know how to load .doc files into an appropriate application. The applications used are:

- Word processor
- Publishing package
- Presentation package
- Spreadsheet
- Database

All images are provided as .jpg files.

Skill standard coverage and range	Where to find it
1.1.1 use ICT to plan and organise work	• all of the tasks • online worksheet – solving data handling tasks using ICT
1.2.1 select and use software applications to meet needs and solve straightforward problems	• files for most tasks are provided as .doc files. The candidate has to decide which application to load the .doc files into • online worksheet – solving data handling tasks using ICT
1.2.2 select and use interface features effectively to meet needs	• implied in several chapters and tasks
1.2.3 adjust system settings as appropriate to individual needs	• online worksheet
1.3.1 work with files, folders and other media to access, organise, store, label and retrieve information	• chapter 12
1.4.1 demonstrate how to create, use and maintain secure passwords	• online worksheet
1.4.2 demonstrate how to minimise the risk of computer viruses	• chapter 4 (email safety)
1.5.1 search engines, queries	• chapter 4 (search engine) • chapter 10 (AND, OR, NOT and logical operators) • chapter 6 (filtering)
1.6.1 recognise and take account of currency, relevance, bias and copyright when selecting and using information	• relevance of information covered in most chapters • currency, bias and copyright in online worksheet
1.7.1 apply editing, formatting and layout techniques to meet needs, including text, tables, graphics, records, numbers, charts, graphs or other digital content	• formatting covered in many chapters and tasks • chapter 12 (tables) • chapter 7 (charts and graphs) • chapter 9 (graphics)
1.8.1 process numerical data	• chapter 6
1.8.2 display numerical data in a graphical format	• chapter 7
1.8.3 use field names and data types to organise information	• chapter 10

Skill standard coverage and range	Where to find it
1.8.4 enter, search, sort and edit records	• chapters 6, 10 and 11
1.9.1 read, send and receive electronic messages with attachments	• In many tasks • chapter 4
1.9.2 demonstrate understanding of the need to stay safe and respect others when using ICT-based communication	• chapter 4
1.10.1 for print and for viewing on screen	• chapter 1 (posters) • chapter 2 (leaflets) • chapter 3 (newsletters) • chapter 5 (presentations) • letters, flyers, information sheets and invitations covered by some tasks and in online material
1.10.2 check for accuracy and meaning	• online worksheets
1.11.1 evaluate own use of ICT tools	• at each stage of a task and at the task's completion students should be asked to reflect on whether they feel they used the best, most efficient approach • discussion with peers and teachers is encouraged • see online document
2.1.1 use ICT to plan and analyse complex or multi-step tasks and activities and to make decisions about suitable approaches	• implied in the tasks, practice will help with this skill • online worksheet helps with planning and suitable approaches
2.2.1 select and use software applications to meet needs and solve complex problems	• skill developed through talking tasks • online worksheet for choosing software
2.2.2 select and use a range of interface features and system facilities effectively to meet needs	• implied within most chapters
2.2.3 select and adjust system settings as appropriate to individual needs	• online worksheet
2.2.4 respond to ICT problems and take appropriate action	• online worksheet
2.2.5 understand the danger of computer viruses and how to minimise risk	• chapter 4
2.3.1 manage files, folders and other media storage to enable efficient information retrieval	• chapter 12
2.4.1 search engines, queries and AND/NOT/OR, >,<,>=,<=, contains, begins with, use of wild cards	• chapters 4, 6 and 10
2.5.1 recognise and take account of copyright and other constraints on the use of information	• online worksheet
2.5.2 evaluate fitness for purpose of information	• chapters 1, 2, 3 and 5
2.6.1 apply a range of editing, formatting and layout techniques to meet needs, including text, tables, graphics, records, numerical data, charts, graphs or other digital content	• covered in many chapters • chapter 12 (tables) • online worksheet (tables) • chapter 9 (diagrams and logos)
2.7.1 process and analyse numerical data	• chapters 6 and 8

Skill standard coverage and range	Where to find it
2.7.2 display numerical data in an appropriate graphical format	• chapter 7
2.7.3 use appropriate field names and data types to organise information	• chapter 10
2.7.4 analyse and draw conclusions from a data set by searching, sorting and editing records	• chapters 10 and 11
2.8.1 organise electronic messages, attachments and contacts	• chapter 4 • online worksheets
2.8.2 use collaborative tools appropriately	• online worksheet
2.8.3 understand the need to stay safe and to respect others when using ICT-based communication	• chapter 4
2.9.1 organise and integrate information of different types to achieve a purpose, using accepted layouts and conventions as appropriate	• chapters 1, 2, 3 and 5 • online worksheets
2.9.2 work accurately and check accuracy, using software facilities where appropriate	• covered in tasks and most chapters
2.10.1 evaluate the selection, use and effectiveness of ICT tools and facilities used to present information	• at each stage of a task and at the task's completion students should be asked to reflect on whether they feel they used the best, most efficient approach • discussion with peers and teachers is encouraged

A poster is a *visual* presentation of information and should be designed as such – you must not simply reproduce your written text in poster format. When developing posters, most people try to pack as much as they can onto the page. Instead, you should focus on making the most important information stand out and not try to include too much.

A poster should be understandable to the reader without the need for other information – people might look at it as they pass by; you need to catch their attention.

> Keep it simple

Do not try to do too much with your poster – the fewer words you use, the better. Obviously this is not a hard and fast rule, but it is a good guideline. Many people use far too many words because they try to say too much with their poster. Decide what your message is and focus on it. Don't add anything that does not contribute to your message.

A good poster	A bad poster
All elements, even the figure legends, are visible from 1 metre away.	Objective(s) and main point(s) are hard to find.
Good organisation – the main headings explain the points.	Poor organisation – it's hard to find the key message.
Indicates the relative importance of elements graphically – each main point is stated in large typeface headings; details are subordinated visually, using smaller typefaces.	Text is too small or there is too much text.
Displays the essential content (the messages) in the title, main headings and graphics.	Graphics are poor.

> Think about the audience

Who is your poster intended for? Think about words, colours and images appropriate for the audience you want to attract.

To design a poster you must first answer some key questions.

Purpose of the poster	• What do you want to achieve? • What message do you want to get across? • Who is your target audience?
Plan the layout	• Think about headings and subheadings. • Organise the information into sections. • Think about balance and simplicity. • Decide where you want to add images, photographs, graphs, logos etc. • Do not try to present too much detail – less is more in a poster; you need to add what is *important*. • Leave enough white space – don't clutter the poster; it should have a clean and simple layout. • Give contact details for people who might want to follow up the information in the poster.

> Colour

Obviously, using colour on your posters can be very effective. However, how much colour and what types of colour you use are very important. You do not want to overwhelm the viewer with all kinds of colours. Instead, use specific colours that you choose to highlight your best aspects. And use those colours sparingly, with the focus on emphasising the impact parts of your poster.

If you are choosing colours for your poster, remember that certain colours, like some yellows and pinks, are very difficult to see and read. Text and background colours should complement or contrast with each other. Make sure your foreground colour (text) is clear when combined with the background colour.

This combination is very gentle on the eyes – but very soft and hard to read from a distance.

This combination is also gentle on the eyes – black is often the best colour to use for text because it is easy to see from a distance.

This combination puts a lot of strain on the eyes and is very hard to read.

This combination also strains the eyes.

> Text

Text size and font type are very important aspects of designing a poster. They determine whether or not your audience will be able to read your poster with ease.

Make sure the text you use is big enough to be read easily from a reasonable distance. As a general rule, you should be able to read your poster easily from a distance of about 1.5 metres. The text size you use on your poster will be determined by the type of font you use, but a font size of about 36 to 40 points is usually good. This is especially important if your target customers include people who may have vision problems (such as the elderly).

Choose a font type that is easy to read, as shown in the following examples.

Arial font is clear and clean and is easy-to-read.

Courier font might be easy to read, but is one of the oldest, more boring fonts around.

Italic fonts are not always easy to read, especially on a poster, where people must read from a distance!

It is not easy to read words that are in capital letters – but sometimes this is used to make something like a heading stand out. For example,

POSTER HEADING

> Poster heading

Generally avoid using all capital letters, except for the title. The emphasis of capital letters helps titles to stand out, but 'all caps' takes longer to read than mixed upper and lowercase letters.

There is no secret code for making a great poster – using these tips will give you a good start. You want your poster to speak to your target customers and tell them what you want them to know. Avoid italicised or fancy scripts. Highlighting with colours or underlining important information is acceptable, but make sure your font style is consistent over the entire poster. Don't use too many font styles.

There are recommended font sizes to use on an A4 poster – you will need to double these on an A3 poster:

Main title	50 points	at least 2 cm high
Subheadings	25 points	0.5–1.0 cm high
Body text	14 points	0.25–0.5 cm high

> Poster tasks

Now that you know what makes a good poster, here are some examples of how you can use some of this knowledge. You can find all the files needed on the website at www.hodderplus.co.uk/ocrictfunctionalskills.

Possible answers to all the tasks in the book can be found on the website. Your poster may not look exactly the same because everyone approaches a task in a slightly different way, but your poster should contain the same information in roughly the same position and fill the page.

> Matt is going to hold a car boot sale to raise funds for the Hartwell Football Club youth team. He wants you to design a poster to advertise the car boot sale.
>
> Matt has provided you with some written information that he wants included in the poster. He has also provided some images.

The first decision is what software to use to produce the poster. The choice is usually between a word processor and a publishing package. This particular poster can be produced using a word processor.

Matt has provided the following files for you to use:
- HFC logo image
- HFC poster text

Car Boot Sale

organised by Hartwell Football Club

at Hartwell Football Club ground, Main
Road, Hartwell

on Saturday 10th May

To book a stall ring Matt on 01222 123456

We are raising money for the Hartwell
Football Club youth team

Turn out your garages and lofts

Sell your stuff

Find bargains

This text and image must be used and arranged appropriately. An idea of the kind of poster you could have produced is shown in Figure 1.1. Look at this sample poster and try to find the main information.

Would you know:
- where to go for the car boot sale?
- when it was to be held?
- who to contact?

A very important piece of information is missing from the poster – what is it? Matt has forgotten to include the starting time and closing time!

Figure 1.1 Car boot sale poster

Task 1.1 (Level 1) > > > > >

1 Copy the poster in Figure 1.1 using a word processor.
2 Include the starting time of 2 p.m. and the closing time of 6 p.m. in an appropriate place on the poster.
3 Save your poster using a sensible filename – such as **Car boot sale poster**.
4 Print out the poster on an A4 sheet.

Matt has provided the following files:

- HFC poster text
- HFC logo image

Evidence required

- A printout of the poster on an A4 sheet.
- A screen dump showing where the files are stored.

Task 1.2 (Level 1) > > > > >

The car boot sale was such a success that Matt decides to hold another one. He learned a few things from organising the first sale and is going to try to make more money with this one.

Matt has asked you to produce a poster for the Hartwell Football Club.

1 Create the poster for Matt using the text and image files provided.
2 Include the table of prices in the poster – the prices are shown below.
3 Make sure that the text, images and table are formatted appropriately and that the words 'football net' are removed from the image of the football net.

Type of charge	Price
Each car	£5.00
Table space inside	£8.00
Table space outside	£3.00

4 Save your poster using a suitable filename.
5 Make sure that the poster fits on an A4 sheet. Print your poster.

Matt has provided the following files:

- HFC poster text
- HFC logo image
- Football net image

Evidence required

- A printout of the poster on an A4 sheet.
- A screen dump showing where the files are stored.

Task 1.3 (Level 2) > > > > >

Chris is a member of a group who are trying to save a colony of seals.

He is organising a jumble sale to help raise funds for the Save-a-Seal campaign.

He has asked you to produce a poster which could be copied and displayed in the town to advertise the jumble sale. He has given you some information that he would like to include on the poster.

Choose software suitable for creating an A4 poster and then:

1 Create the poster for Chris using the text and image provided.
2 Include the 'seal facts' table at the bottom of the poster. You will have to use the seal information sheet provided on the website to find the facts for the table.

Seal facts				
	Males		Females	
	Length	Weight	Length	Weight
Grey seal				
Common seal				

3 Save your poster using a suitable filename.
4 Make sure that the poster fits on an A4 sheet. Print your poster.

Chris has provided the following files:

- Seal poster text
- Seal image
- Seal information sheet

Evidence required

- A printout of the poster on an A4 sheet.
- A screen dump showing where the files are stored.

John needs a poster for a school disco. The poster needs to fit on one A4 sheet.

John has provided the disco information text and some images.

1　Create the poster for John.
2　You should save any files you create so it is clear to John what is in them.

Evidence required

- A printout of the poster on an A4 sheet.
- A screen dump showing where any files created are stored.

> Finally

As you go home today, look around at the posters you come across.
- Are they good posters?
- Do they convey the information you need?
- Are they easy to read?
- Are they attractive?
- As a result of looking at the poster, are you tempted to do or buy what is advertised?

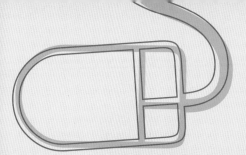

Chapter 2
Designing a leaflet

Please note: this chapter is aimed at level 2 students. Leaflets are not required at level 1.

Leaflets are both visual and informative. They should look attractive enough to encourage people to read them, but also deliver the information required.

Leaflets are made up of one sheet of A4, printed on both sides (recto and verso) and folded into several display panels of text with images. You need to decide the best way to fold your leaflet before designing it – see Figures 2.1 and 2.2.

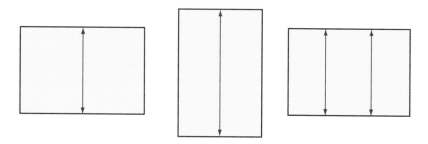

Figure 2.1 **Simple folds**

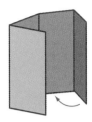

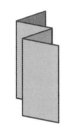

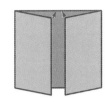

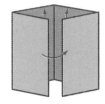

Roll fold
Has two or more parallel folds which fold in on each other.

Concertina fold
The paper zig-zags like a concertina.

Open gate fold
The two parallel folds fold in to meet in the middle without overlapping.

Closed gate fold
The two parallel folds fold in to meet in the middle without over-lapping. Then the brochure folds at the middle.

Figure 2.2 More complicated folds

Leaflets can contain more information than simple advertisements – but they should still be worded carefully and have appropriate graphics and headings. Leaflets are simple but effective promotional tools for businesses and other organisations. Uses include corporate information, single project information, information from an organisation, such as a DIY store or the NHS describing safety tips or giving support advice on a medical condition, promoting an event or publicising an action.

Leaflets are not necessarily read front to back, beginning to end. People often pick them up and browse from the back or the middle, or glance at them quickly on their way to the bin. Therefore every section of a leaflet should be eye-catching and informative.

> Keep it simple

Leaflets are not designed for in-depth studies or complicated arguments. They should be kept simple to get their message across as easily and understandably as possible.

A good leaflet	A bad leaflet
Presents one message so the reader is clear about the point of the leaflet.	Presents too much information and just ends up confusing the reader.
Is organised into sections of coherent information under a heading or subheading.	Is poorly organised with too much text that takes time to read.
Headings and subheadings inform the reader of the following paragraph's content.	Confusing headings.
Has good quality and relevant images to support the text.	Uses poor quality images, or none.
Has attractive graphics in the headings and subheadings to attract the eye.	Graphics are poor.

> Think about the audience

Who is your leaflet for? Think about appropriate words, colours, images for the audience you want to attract.

To design a leaflet you must first answer some key questions.

Purpose of the leaflet	<ul><li>What do you want to achieve?</li><li>What message do you want to get across?</li><li>Who is your target audience?</li><li>Why use a leaflet?</li></ul>
Plan the layout	<ul><li>You'll need headings and subheadings.</li><li>Organise the information into sections.</li><li>Keep it simple.</li><li>Avoid long sentences.</li><li>Don't go into too much detail.</li><li>Decide where you want to add images, photographs, graphs, logos, etc.</li><li>Provide contact details for people who want to follow up the information.</li></ul>

> Colour

The amount of colour you use will depend on the budget you have for printing your leaflet. The more colour you have, the more expensive the printing. Don't overload your text with colour. You will attract readers with coherent colour use for headings and subheadings, but too much will look unprofessional and your leaflet will end up, unread, in the bin. If you're on a budget and will be merely photocopying the leaflet, stick to black and white. You should print on good quality, fairly stiff paper to make the best impression.

> Text

Use a font that is easy to read. Remember your target audience – if it's likely to be the aged, use a bigger font because they cannot read small text. You can use a different font for headings and you can make it bigger than the text in paragraphs. Never write text in capital letters – use only for headings.

> Language

Keep your leaflet language concise, simple and grammatically correct. Avoid long sentences – remember, you are trying to entice your reader to read on. Long sentences will lose their attention, and people don't read them. Use bullets to make points stand out.

If your leaflet is a promotional one for a commercial company, slip 'power words' into the text such as 'free', 'exciting', 'exclusive', 'win', 'bargain', 'bonus' and so on. Make your reader want to take action by following up with 'Buy before (date) and receive a gift', or '10% off' as closing lines.

> Design

Decide how you will fold the leaflet. This will affect where the first and last panels are, and how you place the text on the others.

- **Leaflet heading** – use capital letters or a large font for the title. Make it snappy and stand out so it grabs your reader's attention. The front panel should be visually attractive with images, logo and symbol.
- **Subheadings** – use a bold font, nothing too fancy, and make sure the headings describe what follows so that a reader who just has time to scan the leaflet will still be left with a good idea of the content.
- **Text** – make sure you have all the documentation you need to complete your text. Make the progress of the text logical and check for accuracy.
- **Images** – add images that are relevant to the text to reinforce the message but make sure that they print well.
- **Space** – you don't need to fill every panel; blank space makes a leaflet easier to read.

A leaflet may also be called a rotat (or news sheet), which is like a mini newspaper and may contain the activities of a club. It is usually issued on a regular basis such as once a month

An information sheet is produced by an organisation to describe something such as a statue or historic battleground or 'how to join our club'.

A brochure is often produced by businesses and will contain information on services offered, prices and contact details.

> Leaflet tasks (Level 2)

Now that you have seen what makes a good leaflet, here are some examples of how you could use some of this knowledge. You can find all the files needed on the website at www.hodderplus.co.uk/ocrictfunctionalskills.

> Carol has a bed and breakfast business using the two spare bedrooms in her house. She has asked you to design a leaflet to advertise her business.
>
> Carol has provided you with some written information that she wants included in the leaflet. She has also provided some images.

Carol has provided a picture of her house and a map …

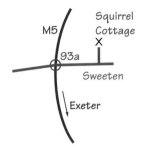

and some text:

> Carol would like to welcome you to Squirrel Cottage Bed &
> Breakfast, her lovely period home in the North Bedminster
> village of Sweeten. Situated in a unique central position to the
> major towns, cities and areas of outstanding beauty in the region,
> Squirrel Cottage is ideal for the tourist and business visitor alike.
>
> Whatever the reason for your visit, you can always be
> assured a warm reception, quality accommodation, excellent
> hospitality and superb home cooked food using local
> produce. Many visitors return time and again.

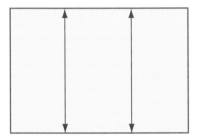

Figure 2.3

The leaflet will be printed on one side of A4 paper and folded as shown in Figure 2.3.

A publishing package would be best to use for creating a leaflet because they have many templates already set up. A word processor could be used if you do not have a publisher.

An idea of the kind of leaflet you could have produced is shown in Figure 2.4.

Squirrel Cottage

Carol would like to welcome you to Squirrel Cottage Bed & Breakfast, her lovely period home in the North Bedminster village of Sweeten. Situated in a unique central position to the major towns, cities and areas of outstanding beauty in the region, Squirrel Cottage is ideal for the tourist and business visitor alike.

Whatever the reason for your visit, you can always be assured a warm reception, quality accommodation, excellent hospitality and superb home cooked food using local produce. Many visitors return time and again.

How to find us

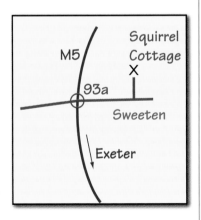

Figure 2.4 Come to Squirrel Cottage

Task 2.1 (Level 2) > > > > >

1 Create a copy of the leaflet for Carol.
2 Include the contact details for Carol Smith above the words 'How to find us'. You can find Carol's contact details in the text of the leaflet.
3 Print out using a landscape A4 sheet, and fold the leaflet appropriately.

Carol has provided the following files:

- Squirrel Cottage text
- Squirrel Cottage image
- Squirrel Cottage map image

Evidence required

- A printout of the leaflet on an A4 sheet.
- A screen dump showing where the files are stored.

Task 2.2 (Level 2) > > > > >

Carol Smith of Squirrel Cottage gets all the eggs for her bed and breakfast guests from Tall Hill Farm, which produces free range eggs. John Griggs is proud of his happy hens and would like a leaflet made to explain his produce.

1 Create a leaflet for John similar to the one created for Carol in Task 1, but without the map.
2 John has provided you with a list of egg prices he would like included in an appropriate place in the leaflet. This is shown in Figure 2.5.
3 Print out your leaflet.

John has provided three files for you to use:

- Tall Hill Farm information text
- Farm contact details
- Hens image

Evidence required

- A printout of the leaflet on an A4 sheet.
- A screen dump showing where the files are stored.

Egg prices

10 large	£2.75
10 medium	£2.45
10 small	£2.00
6 mixed	£1.50

Figure 2.5 Egg price list

Can you think of any ways that the leaflet on the website could be improved or what might be added? Next time you see a leaflet, think about what is on it and how it is presented. You might be able to use those ideas one day yourself.

Task 2.3 (Level 2) > > > > >

Wayne runs a hotel where anglers can come and spend time fishing for pleasure in one of the three small lakes in the hotel's private grounds.

Wayne has asked you to produce a leaflet to help him to advertise his hotel. The hotel is called The Angler's Paradise. It is situated in Lake Lane, Sweeten, North Bedminster.

Wayne has sketched out the design of the leaflet as shown in Figure 2.6.

1 Choose a suitable application and create the leaflet for Wayne. Make sure you use all the files available.
2 Wayne would like to include some information about different types of fish – he has not provided the images. Use the internet to find images of the following to insert with the **types of fish** text:
   - perch
   - bream
3 Save your leaflet using an appropriate filename.
4 Print out your leaflet.

Wayne has provided the following files to use:

- Hotel information text
- Hotel contact details text
- Types of fish text
- Hotel image
- Lakes image

Evidence required

- A printout of the leaflet on an A4 sheet.
- A screen dump showing where the files are stored.

Figure 2.6 Wayne's sketches

Kylie runs a window cleaning business. She needs a leaflet to advertise her business.

Kylie needs the leaflet to fit on both sides of one A4 sheet.

1 Create the leaflet for Kylie.
2 Save the leaflet file so that Kylie can easily find it.

Kylie has provided you with the following files:

- Company history text
- Contact details text
- Information text
- Window cleaning girl image
- Window cleaning image 1
- Window cleaning image 2
- Window cleaning image 3
- Window cleaning image 4

Evidence required

- A printout of the leaflet on an A4 sheet.
- A screen dump showing where the file is stored.

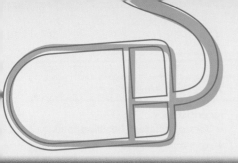

Chapter 3
Creating a newsletter

Newsletters are distributed regularly. They usually focus on a main topic that is of interest to people who want to receive it – these people are called subscribers. Many different organisations produce newsletters – including clubs, businesses, companies, church groups, and associations. They can be made available as paper copies or electronic copies that are often sent by email.

> What makes a good newsletter?

The first thing you need to consider is the newsletter's title. This needs to show the purpose of the newsletter, and allow people to recognise immediately where it is from, inviting them to open it up and read it. It should be easy to remember and spell. Electronic newsletters often even include the reader's name. Newsletters work best if they are sent out regularly.

You should design newsletters using the three Cs:

- **Consistency** – making the newsletter look the same each time so that users recognise it.
- **Conservation** – reducing the number of words keeps the newsletter short and to the point. Don't make it too lengthy – people won't read it.
- **Contrast** – making the newsletter attractive and interesting helps to produce an attention-grabbing document, which will keep the reader interested. While nothing replaces good content, good design is very important in newsletters. Use colours and contrast to draw the reader's eye. If you are advertising special offers, try to emphasise that part of the newsletter.

A good newsletter	A bad newsletter
Is consistent: • clear headline fonts • good text fonts • relevant photos • one image caption style • designed on the same template each time.	Inconsistency: • lots of different headline fonts • too many text fonts • irrelevant images and graphics • a change in look for every issue.
Uses: • a maximum of three fonts • easily readable fonts • limited boxes and frames • limited graphics.	Clutter: • fonts chosen for visual impact, not readability • every article is inside a box or fancy frame • distracting graphics cover every space.
Has contrast: • headline fonts – sans serif • text fonts – serif • size – make the headline really big • text/white space – wide margins around long articles • text colour – reverse text/ background styles (light on dark) • variable text alignment • supersize one graphic.	A lack of contrast resulting in: • a boring-looking document • nothing standing out • all articles look the same • conflict between content and design – serious content/flippant design elements.

> Think about the audience

Who is the intended audience of your newsletter? Think about appropriate words, colours, images for the audience you want to attract. Is the newsletter to be formal or informal? Would their first impression of the newsletter be the right one?

To design a newsletter, you must first consider the following:

Purpose of the newsletter	• What do you want to achieve? • What message do you want to get across? • Who is your target audience? • Are you seeking to inform, entertain, promote a product, generate sales?
Plan the layout	• Name of the newsletter in the nameplate. • Date of publication. • Number of columns. • Different zones of text for short and longer articles. • Size of headings and subheadings for articles. • A masthead to identify publisher, contributors, contact information. • Number of images and graphics. • A mix of images and text. • Where to put the by-line (the name of the writer).

> Layout

Use grids to set a structure to the page. Many newsletters use grids of three columns which are the most flexible for varying content.

Photos can be set within a column, or over two or even three columns. Headlines can be adjusted similarly according to the length and importance of an article. A major story would have a long headline that stretches over two columns.

A good layout will help the reader to see what is most important, and to navigate from one article to another easily.

> Graphics

Images should be chosen with care so they illustrate or support the text. An image can be re-sized if it helps.

Backgrounds don't have to be white, they can be coloured, shaded or even contain a secondary image printed faintly to cover some dead white space.

Use a logo which could be placed next to the nameplate to give the name of the organisation more impact.

> Content

The content of a newsletter depends very much on the organisation producing it. However, there are certain types of content to be considered whatever the category.

These include:

- hard news for articles about what's been going on, company successes, important issues, and any other newsworthy item
- editorials for the editor to discuss an issue
- regular columns relevant to the newsletter's content and audience
- advertising to help pay for publication costs.

They might also include:

- new feature updates
- member highlights
- employee interviews
- seasonal topics
- company statistics.

Whatever the type of newsletter, content is important. Write, edit and rewrite articles until they are free of factual and grammatical errors, are easily read and are interesting. An interesting newsletter that is well designed will attract readers, who will come back again and again, developing readership loyalty.

> Newsletter tasks

Now that you have seen what makes a good newsletter, here are some examples of how you could use some of this knowledge. You can find all the files needed on the website at www.hodderplus. co.uk/ocrictfunctionalskills.

George Bunting is the editor of the Chestpury Local History Society. Each month George has to write a newsletter for the society. For the March issue, No. 25, he has collected the following:
- an article from Carole Read about a trip to Gloucester with some pictures
- an advertisement for window cleaning
- an advertisement for an equestrian shop
- information about membership fees
- details of the next meeting
- a quiz.

George has asked you to help in creating the March newsletter. The newsletter will use both sides of an A4 sheet. George has produced the first page of the newsletter as shown in Figure 3.1.

Figure 3.1 The Chestpury newsletter

He would like you to produce the second page – this should include information and articles not included on the first page. It should use similar fonts and styles including the use two columns. Include the information that the next meeting will be held on Thursday 29th of April. Include a suitable image with the announcement of the prize for the quiz.

Task 3.1 (Level 1) > > > > >

1 Using the files provided and the image shown in Figure 3.1, reproduce page 1 of the newsletter.
2 Print the page.

George used the following files:

- Next meeting text
- Window cleaning ad image
- Visit to Gloucester text
- Cathedral image
- Bishop Hooper image

3 Produce the second page of the newsletter for George. Make sure you include all the missing information. George would like the membership fees included as a table. Include a suitable image to go with the quiz prize.
4 Save the newsletter file using a sensible name so that George can find it.

George has provided the following files for you to use:

- Membership fees text
- Harry Potter text
- Old house image
- Equestrian ad image
- Quiz text

Evidence required

- A printout of the first page of the newsletter on an A4 sheet.
- A screen dump showing where the files are stored.
- A printout of the second page of the newsletter on an A4 sheet.
- A screen dump showing where the files are stored.

Task 3.2 (Level 1) (examination type task) > > > > >

Geocaching involves hunting for a hidden cache following clues and map co-ordinates. The cache usually consists of a notebook to sign, though it may contain clues to other caches and objects to be transferred to another location. Discoveries are logged on the internet for all geocachers to read.

Sheila has been interested in the sport of geocaching for some time. She and her friends enjoy the mixture of orienteering, exercise and treasure hunting. Sheila wants to issue a one-page A4 newsletter (just one side of the page) about her friends and their latest geocaching adventures. She has collected some information for the newsletter which she has stored in a folder called 'Geocache'.

1 Use the files that Sheila has collected to produce the newsletter. Make sure it has a suitable title.
2 Save the finished file.
3 Print the newsletter.

She has provided the following files for you to use:

- Hidden cache image
- Travelling football image
- Lone oak tree image
- Hunt text
- Dinner announcement text
- Last meeting text

Evidence required

- A printout of the newsletter on an A4 sheet.
- A screen dump showing where the files are stored.

Task 3.3 (Level 1 or 2) > > > > >

Produce a newsletter on a topic that interests you. You will need to:

- plan the heading and think of a title
- collect some text
- collect some images
- plan how you will combine the text and images

Figure 3.2 shows some possible layouts.

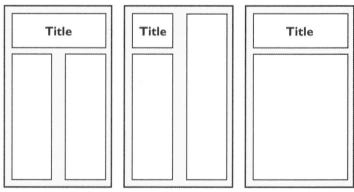

Figure 3.2 Newsletter layouts

Evidence required

- A printout of the newsletter on an A4 sheet.
- A screen dump showing where the files are stored.

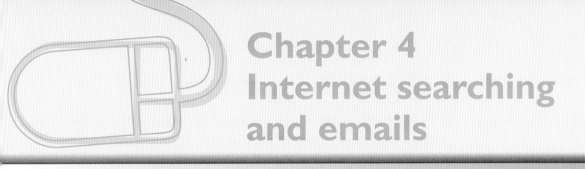

There are hundreds of millions of internet pages. To search for information you need help, and the help at your fingertips is the search engine. There are several search engines available – you may well have heard of Google, Yahoo, AskJeeves and MSN, which are just four of many.

However, using search engines takes a little practice if you are not to get confused by the huge number of hits, or you are unable to find what you want in the small selection that comes up. To make best use of a search engine, you have to use keywords.

> Keywords

A keyword is a word that represents a topic of research. In order to come up with the best keywords, you have to know what it is you are searching for.

For example, you might be asked to think about where you want to go on holiday and what activities you want to do. If you do a search on 'holiday' you'll get back hundreds of millions of answers, or hits.

To refine, or limit, your search you decide that, in fact, you want to go on holiday in the UK, near the sea, where you can search for fossils. Your search would therefore be:

holiday fossils sea uk

The search engine would find only about 300 000 matches – with the most relevant first. Search engines are not case sensitive, so you don't need to worry about capital letters. It makes no difference whether you type 'uk' or 'UK', the search results are the same.

> Phrases

Most search engines don't accept whole phrases or questions and will not take any notice of 'clutter' words such as articles (the, a) and pronouns (he, you, she, this). You should stick to nouns and objects (fossil hunting, electric guitar).

Some search engines allow you to put quotation marks around the phrase – e.g. 'electric guitar' – and this means that the search is done on both words and they must appear in the exact order. This will reduce the number of hits.

> Advanced searches

If you find there are too many irrelevant hits coming up, you can refine your search using the 'Advanced search' window. There is usually a link to this next to the search bar in your search engine as shown in Figure 4.1.

Figure 4.1 **Advanced search**

Clicking on this will open a new window with a form (Figure 4.2) that you can fill in to identify more precisely:

- what you are searching for
- what information you don't want included.

Figure 4.2 **Using an advanced search form**

The first part of the advanced search window contains a number of bars to search for web pages that have the following:

- all these words
- this exact word or phrasing
- any of these words
- none of these words.

For example, you decide you want to find electric guitar lessons online for beginners. In your advanced search engine you could enter in the 'all these words' bar:

electric guitar online lessons beginner

This will return sites containing only documents that have all the keywords or phrases – about 382 000 hits.

This is still too many, so you go back to the advanced search form, cut the words from the **all these words** bar and paste them in the **this exact wording or phrase** bar. When you click on 'Search', the number of hits that come back will be much smaller – maybe 2.

Your friends are planning to go to a pop concert in either Manchester or Birmingham and want to know where to go and what's on.

For this search, enter in the **this exact phrase** bar the words 'pop concert'. Then in the **any of these words** bar, 'manchester' or 'birmingham'. As there are Manchesters and Birminghams in the US, you could also put 'UK' in the **all these words** bar. This will return documents that contain UK pop concert information for Manchester or Birmingham – something like 8200 hits.

While you're there, you decide it would be fun to visit some of the things to see, but you are not interested in museums, art galleries or theatres. You can add these constraints to the **none of these words** bar. If you want to know what's on for children, Figure 4.3 shows what your advanced search would look like. It would return about 169 000 hits.

For the latest information, you could restrict the date range of the web pages to the last 30 days.

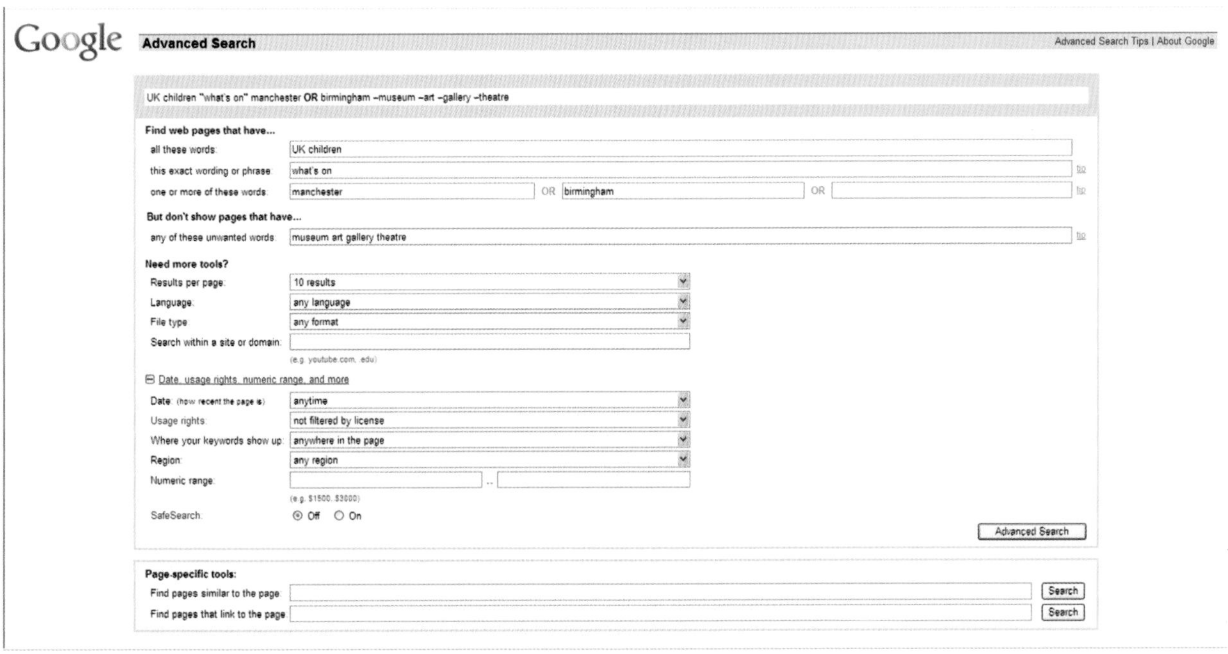

Figure 4.3 **A very specific search**

Summary

- Think about what you are searching for.
- Use relevant keywords – nouns, objects.
- Don't use 'clutter' words ('a', 'the', 'she').
- Check your spelling.
- Use several keywords to refine your search.
- Check the 'Help' file for your search engine's Boolean operators.

Remember, a good search will return more relevant information and save you time by reducing the number of pages of hits. Using a search engine is a skill, and the more you practise the better you'll be at it.

> Emails

Electronic mail, or email, sends messages over the internet almost instantly. You can no longer do business effectively if you do not have an email address. Families and friends also use it to keep in contact cheaply and easily.

This is what you need to send an email:

- a computer
- an internet connection
- an email address
- the email address of the recipient.

There are many free internet-based email providers such as Yahoo, Hotmail, Gmail. If you have an internet service provider such as Orange, Talk Talk, BT, or AOL it will also offer email addresses for household members.

> Sending an email

Once you are logged into your email provider, click on 'New Message' and fill in the header.

The **header** contains the name and email address of the recipient in the 'TO…' box, plus a 'CC…' box if you want to send a copy of the email to someone else. The 'BCC…' box means 'blind copy' – use this if you want to copy someone in, but don't want the recipient to know that you've sent the email to that person. Getting the spelling of the address right is very important – get it wrong by just one letter and it won't arrive, and you'll end up getting an error message.

Next fill in the **Subject**. It helps the recipient if the subject line gives some idea about what is in the body of the message – especially if they receive a lot of emails. For example, instead of writing 'Party', you could write 'Invitation party 8/5/10'.

The email address of the person the message is being sent to.

CC stands for 'carbon copy'. A copy of the message is sent to this person.

The subject of the message.

The email message, sometimes this is called the 'body'.

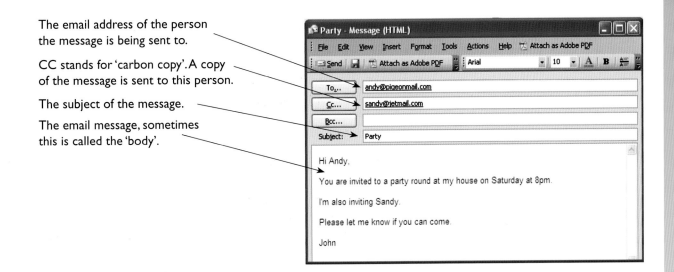

The **body** of the email contains the message that you want to write. Because email is so immediate, people become sloppy about what they write. Email is less formal than letter-writing, but it's different to talking face-to-face. A screen is blank, it gives no indication of the personality or emotion of the writer, and this makes it difficult to understand whether your correspondent is being serious or funny, or is happy or sad. This can make it difficult to communicate effectively and can lead to misunderstandings.

When you are happy that your message can be clearly understood, click on 'Send'.

> Email features

These include:

- adding a signature to your outgoing mail with your name and address, or a quote, or inserting an image
- attaching documents, photos or other files to your message – there is usually a limit to the total size of files you can send
- receiving and opening attachments from others
- creating folders for the emails you receive, to manage them more easily.

> Email safety

Never open an attachment unless you know the sender. Attachments can contain viruses and other malware designed to destroy your computer data and cause chaos. Your email provider should always scan attachments before you open them to check that they are clean.

Use an anonymous free email address if you sign up for a dating or friendship site. Do not give out your full name and use a pseudonym for better protection. If a contact seems suspicious, just ignore the email and delete it from your inbox – do not respond and they'll just go away.

> Respecting others

Emails are very useful. It is possible to send an email to anyone with an email address and to have them receive it almost instantly. The bad news about emails is that once you have pressed the send button it is usually impossible to get it back. Imagine that you had just written an email to your friend in which you say "I think that my boss is an idiot". In your haste to send it you accidently put your boss's email address instead of the address of your friend. Disaster! So never send emails that are nasty or offensive. Respect the person you are writing to and only put down in an email what you are prepared to say to their face.

> Spam

Spam is electronic junk mail – it's impossible to get rid of spam totally, but there are ways to limit how much you get.

- Use the spam filter option on your email provider – this will identify much of it and send it to the 'Junk Mail' folder.
- Set up the email filter so that messages from people not in your address book go straight to 'Junk Mail' – you'll need to check it for new contacts however.
- Never leave your main email address on websites. Designate a free mail address as the one you use as a 'contact' mail. Use your official address for friends and family only.
- Never respond to spam.
- Always click 'No' on websites that ask if you'd like to receive information from their commercial partners.

> Internet searching and email tasks

Now that you have seen what makes a good email, here are some examples of how you can use them.

Sue has been asked to find out some information from the internet for two British libraries.

She has been asked to find the opening and closing times for every day of the week including Sundays. The information needed is for:

- The Kensington Science Museum Library (London)
- The British Library Reading Registration Office (London)

For internet searching tasks, you will be asked to provide evidence of making the search. This should consist of a screen dump (Figure 4.4) of the search that you carried out.

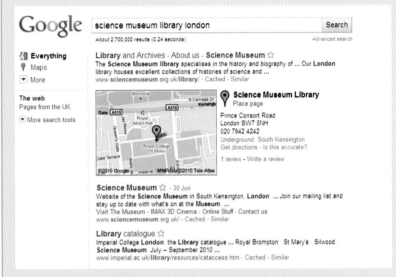

Figure 4.4 Evidence of a search for the Science Museum Library

Sue has been asked to present her results as a table and then to email the table as an attachment to her friend Katy. Katy's email address is katy@ fiction.coz.

Sue searches the internet and finds the information she needs. The information is shown in Figures 4.5a and 4.5b.

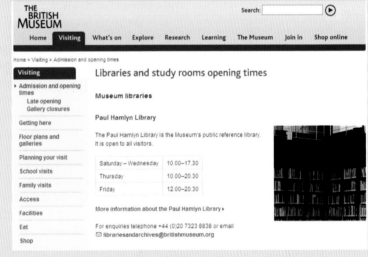

Figure 4.5a Opening and closing times found by Sue for the British Museum

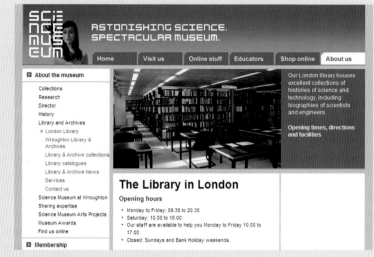

Figure 4.5b Opening and closing times found by Sue for the
Science Museum

Sue creates the table shown below.

	Science Museum Library		British Museum Reader Registration	
Day	Open	Close	Open	Close
Monday	09.30	20.30	10.00	17.30
Tuesday	09.30	20.30	10.00	17.30
Wednesday	09.30	20.30	10.00	17.30
Thursday	09.30	20.30	10.00	20.30
Friday	09.30	20.30	12.00	20.30
Saturday	10.00	18.00	10.00	17.30
Sunday	Closed all day			

Sue saves the table she has made and sends it as an attachment to Katy –
the evidence for this is shown in Fig. 4.6.

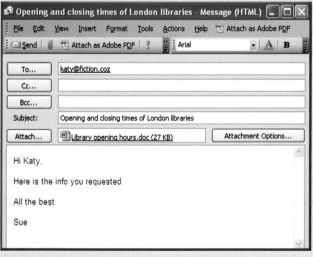

Figure 4.6 Sue's email to Katy

Task 4.1 (Level 1) > > > > >

1 Look on the internet to find the information that Sue found about the library opening and closing times. Check them carefully because they may have changed.
2 Make a table like Sue's and include the up-to-date opening and closing times.
3 Save the table with a suitable filename.
4 Print the table.
5 Attach the file to an email – but do not send it.

Evidence required

- A printout of the table on an A4 sheet.
- A screen dump showing where the table is stored.
- Screen dumps of evidence of searches for:
    British Museum Library opening times
    Science Museum Library opening times
- A screen dump of an email with an attachment.

Task 4.2 (Level 2) > > > > >

Steve is conducting a survey of the numbers of web pages he finds when he carries out a search. He wants to compare the number of hits when he types in mountain gorillas with 'mountain gorillas'. He has asked you to help with the research – Steve has asked you to copy the table shown below and to use the internet to find the results.

Search engine used	Number of hits	
	mountain gorillas	'mountain gorillas'
Google		
Yahoo		
Bing		
Ask Jeeves		

1 Copy Steve's table.
2 Show evidence of one of the searches carried out.
3 Find the information and include it in the table.
4 Produce two separate pie charts to show the comparisons clearly.
5 Save your work so that Steve will be able to find the files at a later date.
6 Print the table, and then the pie charts.

Evidence required

- A printout of the table on an A4 sheet.
- A screen dump of the search results.
- A screen dump showing where the table is stored.
- A printout of the two pie charts.

1 Olu is taking his family to Florida for a once-in-a-lifetime holiday. While he is there he wants to visit the Epcot Centre and find the Mission Space exhibition.
2 Use the internet to find a map of the Epcot theme park for Olu and mark the position of the Mission Space Pavilion on the map.
3 Save the map using a suitable filename so that Olu can find it easily.
4 Produce a screen dump of any searches you carried out.
5 Provide a printout of the map for Olu.

Evidence required

- A screen dump of evidence of searching for maps.
- A screen dump of the map of the Epcot theme park with Mission Space Pavilion marked.
- A screen dump showing where your files are saved.

Chapter 5
Presentations

Presentation software is widely used as a support when you have to give a talk on something. You may have to report on sales figures, the progress of a project, research findings etc. Or maybe sell an idea such as an advertising plan or a new invention to a manufacturer.

There are many different reasons why you would use presentation software, but the most effective presentations all follow similar simple rules – the golden rule is:

● the attention span of most people is very limited, so restrict the amount of information you give and avoid details – they won't be remembered anyway.

> Keep it simple

Don't cram too much information onto slides. People can't read text and listen to a speaker at the same time, so favour graphs and images over lots of text. A presentation is about highlighting what is most important in your research/project/plan. The details can be given in a written report handed out before or after the presentation.

A good presentation	A bad presentation
All elements, even figure legends, are visible from the back of the audience.	Text too small or too much text.
Good organisation – introduction with overview, discussion, conclusion.	Poor organisation with no structure.
No more than one idea per slide.	More than one idea per slide.
Lists of three bullet points – audiences remember threes.	Long lists with irrelevant information.
Images rather than text – use relevant graphics to illustrate points.	Irrelevant graphics and images.
A minimum number of slides – no more than ten for a five-minute talk.	Too many slides.
Animation is used on content – video or introducing ideas one-by-one.	Too much animation.
Spell-checked and grammatically correct.	Error-strewn.

> Think about the audience

Who is your presentation for? Will the audience be made up of experts and professionals, or will you be talking to people who have no specific knowledge of your subject? This will affect what language you use and how much specific detail you give.

To design a presentation, you must first consider the following:

What is the purpose?	<ul><li>What do you want to achieve?</li><li>What message do you want to get across?</li><li>Who is your target audience?</li></ul>
How should I plan the presentation?	<ul><li>Decide what you want to say.</li><li>Decide what to put on the slides to illustrate your points.</li><li>Limit the number of slides.</li><li>Decide how many images and graphics you want to add.</li></ul>

> Colour

The most effective slides have a pale background and dark text – keep it simple and consistent. You can use different colours for headings and main text, so long as you use the same colours throughout.

> Text

Consider the members of the audience at the back of the room. Choose a sans serif font, like Arial, which is easy to read from anywhere in the room – use letters that are big enough so they can be seen from a distance. Try standing back 3 metres from your screen to see if you can read all the text on your slides.

Use capital letters only for the first page and main headings, and be consistent how you use fonts. Keep the titles short and snappy to attract your audience's attention.

> Illustrations

Prefer graphics to text, but only if they are relevant to your talk. Tables do not work well in presentations, so choose charts, such as pie charts, with clear contrasting colours.

Keep logos and professional footers off slides because they only distract from the presentation. Use real photos for effect – these can be photos of actual items or people, or screenshots.

> Giving the presentation

You will not be asked to give a presentation – this list is just for information.

1 Your appearance should not distract the audience's attention from what you are saying.
2 Speak up – people won't understand you if you mumble.
3 Don't gabble – practice speaking slowly and clearly. Allow a moment for important points to sink in – practice in front of real people and ask for feedback.
4 Prepare your presentation – don't read the slides, they are supposed to be a support not an autocue.
5 Know your topic – prepare for questions that your audience might want to ask.
6 Stick to your allotted time – practice so you don't talk for too long.
7 Speak to your audience, not the slides.
8 Try to move a little as you talk – you can use your hands too.
9 Remember, you are the presentation – not your presentation software.
10 Relax.

> Presentation tasks

Now that you have seen what makes a good presentation, here are some examples of how you could use some of this knowledge. You can find all the files needed on the website at www.hodderplus.co.uk/ocrictfunctionalskills.

Grant is making a presentation about British birds and wants to produce some slides about robins.

He has collected some information about robins and some images. He would like the slides arranged under the following headings:

- territories
- nests
- food
- size of bird

Grant has started off the presentation with the slide shown in Figure 5.1.

Robins – territorial facts

❑ Male and female robins look the same.
❑ They both defend their own territories.
❑ When they pair up in December they begin to tolerate each other.
❑ Robins will attack anything that looks like a bird with a red chest.

Figure 5.1 Grant's first slide

Task 5.1 (Level 1) > > > > >

Complete the presentation for Grant, save the presentation so that Grant can find it and print out the presentation slides.

He has provided the following files:

- Robins facts text
- Robins nest image
- Robin image
- Worms image

Evidence required

- A printout of the presentation slides on A4 sheets.
- A screen dump showing where the files are stored.

Task 5.2 (Level 2) > > > > >

Gill is really excited that she is going on a school trip to Florida. She has been told that one of the activities is swimming with manatees. Nobody going on the trip has ever heard of manatees and some of the parents are worried about the activity. Gill has offered to prepare a presentation of around four slides to show to the parents and participants at the next meeting.

Gills has found some pictures of manatees, but has asked you to use the internet to find out:

- where a manatee lives (its habitat)
- what it eats
- what size is it
- whether it is dangerous or not

1 Use the internet to find the information about manatees that Gill wants.
2 Prepare the presentation for Gill.
3 Use a separate folder to store the facts you have collected.
4 Save the presentation so that Gill can find it easily.

Gill has provided the following files:

- Manatee image
- Not a manatee image

Evidence required

- One or more screen dumps showing how you searched for the manatee information.
- A printout of the presentation slides on A4 sheets.
- A screen dump showing where the files are stored.

Task 5.3 (Level 2) > > > > >

Calum belongs to a gardening club. The members have been testing various dwarf sunflower seeds to see if the plants match the description on the packet.

40 members each grew one of each type of plant and then each member provided Calum with the height of their plants after six weeks. This is an example of the form the members had to fill in.

Pendulbury Gardening Club						
Name of member:				Date:		
Plant	Double dandy	Firecracker	Munchkin	Petite bouquet	Teddy bear	Big smile
Height						

Calum has been recording the results in a spreadsheet (Figure 5.2), but the spreadsheet needs to be finished.

	A	B	C	D	E	F	G	H
1	Sunflower growth after 6 weeks							
2	Double dandy	Firecracker	Munchkin	Petite Bouquet	Teddy Bear	Big Smile		Average heights
3	59	54	51	39	54	28		Double dandy
4	61	63	63	37	68	32		Firecracker
5	62	62	66	39	52	29		Munchkin
6	64	53	50	38	63	25		Petite Bouquet
7	47	70	57	49	63	27		Teddy Bear
8	65	61	50	40	69	29		Big Smile
9	50	68	55	44	68	26		
10	50	65	54	39	66	25		
11	51	62	55	54	61	35		
12	38	63	53	44	53	32		
13	58	70	67	43	68	27		
14								

Figure 5.2 Sunflower growth data

Calum is going to give a talk to the gardening club members. He wants you to help him make a short presentation about the sunflowers and their growth.

1 Insert the missing information in the spreadsheet Sunflower growth.xls. You will find the missing information on the website.
2 Calculate the average height of each type of sunflower and position the results as shown in Figure 5.2.
3 Create a bar chart to compare the average heights of sunflowers after 6 weeks growth.
4 Produce the presentation for Calum.

Calum has provided a number of files:

- Sunflower growth.xls
- Sunflower descriptions text
- Double dandy image
- Firecracker image
- Munchkin image
- Petite bouquet image
- Teddy bear image
- Big smile image

Evidence required

- A printout of the completed spreadsheet.
- A printout of the spreadsheet showing formulas.
- A printout of the presentation slides on A4 sheets.
- A screen dump showing evidence of saving the files sensibly with meaningful filenames.

Task 5.4 (Level 1) (examination type task) > > > > >

Leila is a teacher. She needs some slides about pizzas for a lesson she is giving.

Leila needs you to create some slides that she can show on screen during a lesson. She has provided some text and some images.

You should save your file so that it is clear to Leila where to find it.

1 Enter the text and images Leila has provided into a suitable number of slides.
2 Make sure all the information in the slides is formatted appropriately.

Leila has provided you with the following files:

- Pizza image 1
- Pizza image 2
- Pizza text

Evidence required

- A printout of the slides.
- A screen dump showing where the file is stored.

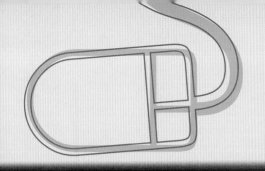

Chapter 6
Spreadsheet functions

SUM   I

COUNT   F

AVERAGE

MIN OR

MAX

Spreadsheets are used for calculating with numbers, and presenting the results of those calculations in a visual format. They are used, for example, by accountants, engineers, bankers, scientists, sales representatives, supermarkets, market researchers and teachers. In fact, anyone who needs to make calculations on profit/loss, financial forecasts, manufacturing designs, results from experiments, sales, commission, data analysis and keeping track of pupil presence and marks. They can also be used at home to monitor household expenses.

When to choose a spreadsheet

One of the best pieces of software for data analysis is a spreadsheet.

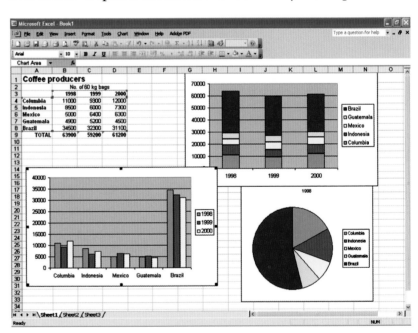

Although you can use a spreadsheet to set up simple tables of textual information, a spreadsheet's real usefulness lies in its ability to calculate using formulas – and to recalculate automatically when values change. They are also ideal when you want to produce a graph to display data. Spreadsheets are great for budgets, financial statements and other tasks that require calculations. Use spreadsheets:

- for simple data entry
- to list and maintain groups of numerically based data

- to carry out calculations and functions on numeric data
- to automatically create charts, which you can then print or import into presentations
- to model data and ask 'what if' type questions.

> Spreadsheet basics

Spreadsheets are made up of **columns**, labelled alphabetically, e.g. A–Z:

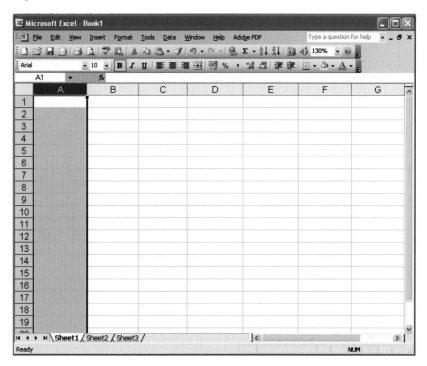

and **rows**, labelled numerically, e.g. 1–100:

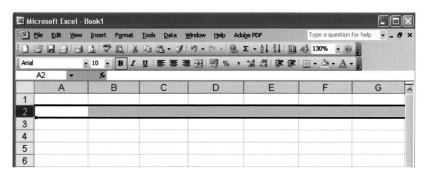

A cell is labelled according to its row number and column letter, e.g.:

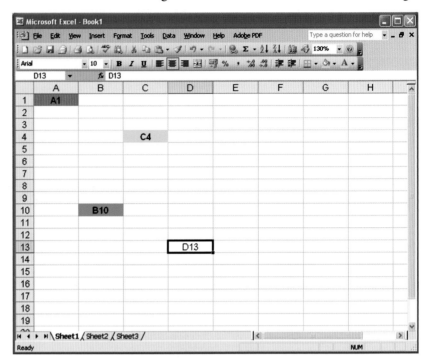

The active cell (the one you're working on) can be identified by the row/column highlights and the border around the cell itself.

> Constructing formulas

At level 1 you will be expected to construct simple formulas using the mathematical operators:

- \+ pronounced "plus" and used for adding
- \- pronounced "minus" and used for taking away
- * pronounced "star or multiplied by" and used for multiplying
- / pronounced "slash or divided by" and used for dividing.

At level 2 you may have to use brackets () to create more complex formulas. Any calculations within a pair of brackets are done first, so brackets help you establish the order in which a formula is solved.

	A	B	C
1	Colour	Number	Price
2	Green	5	£1.20
3	Blue	6	£3.99
4	Red	4	£2.67

A simple formula at level 1 could be the income from the Green
= B2*C2

A complex formula at level 2 could be the income from the Green and Red
=(B2*C2)+(B4*C4)

> Functions

You use functions to perform calculations on data. Spreadsheets have built-in functions to make them easier to use – but you do have to understand what they do exactly.

For level 1 you will need to know about the functions SUM, MIN, MAX. For level 2 you will also need to know how to use AVERAGE, MEDIAN, MODE, IF.

SUM and AutoSUM

The SUM function will add up a row or column of figures. Look at the spreadsheet shown in Figure 6.1 – it gives annual coffee production by the number of 60 kg bags from 1998 to 2000.

To total the column for 1998 you can use the function SUM. In cell B9 you can see the formula for the SUM function: =SUM.

To add a range of numbers, don't type in B4+B5+B6+B7+B8. You can shorten this to B4:B8, which means all the cells from B4 to B8. Note the brackets round the cells – so the whole formula looks like this:

=SUM(B4:B8)

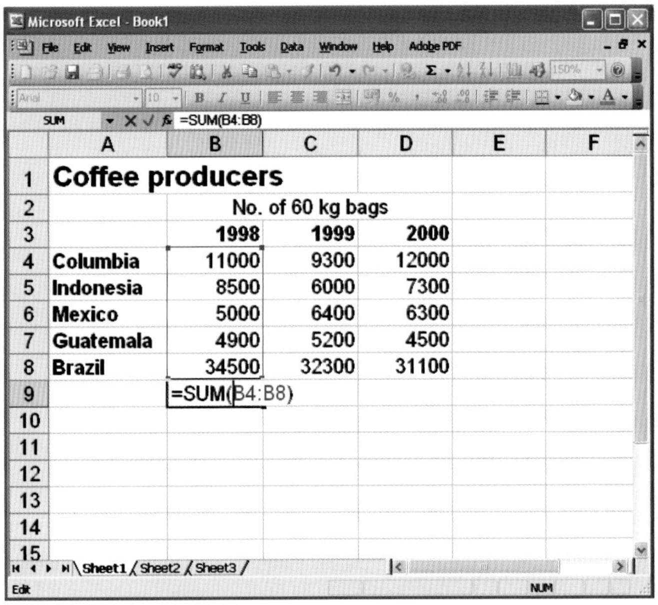

Figure 6.1 **Coffee production data**

Then click on Enter and the total (63 900) will replace the formula in the cell.

The AutoSUM function will also add up a row or column of figures. Its button is in the main toolbar and looks like a Greek capital sigma, Σ.

To use it in this spreadsheet, click cell B9, then click Σ and a grid forms around the range within the column to be calculated. Drag the column to highlight the required figures – don't include the year, for example – and click on Enter. The total will appear in the cell – to identify it, type 'TOTAL' in cell A9 as shown in Figure 6.2.

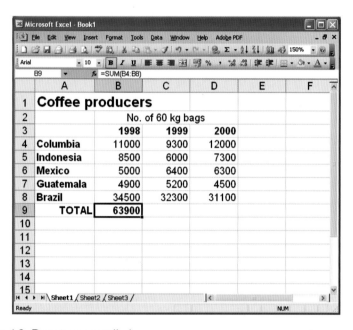

Figure 6.2 **Data items totalled**

You can make the whole row stand out by clicking on the row number 9 and then B (for Bold) button in the main toolbar.

To calculate the number of bags for the other years, the process is even quicker. You'll see a little square on the bottom right-hand corner of cell B9 (see Figure 6.2). When you hover over this square, the cursor turns into a cross. This allows you to drag cell B9 across C9 and D9, which automatically copies the formula in B9 into the other two cells (see Figure 6.3).

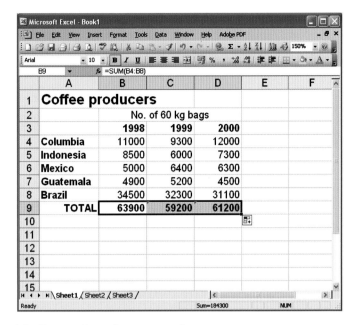

Figure 6.3 **Copying formulas across cells**

You will see the correct totals for 1998, 1999 and 2000 rapidly – and in the correct format.

IF

The IF function is used to find out if the data in a cell is 'true' or 'false'. If it's true, one thing happens; if it's false, a different thing happens. The test looks like this:

=IF(logical_test, value_if_true, value_if_false)

Teachers use this function to find out, for example, how many pupils have passed a test and how many have failed. Figure 6.4 shows the results of a class test.

In this example, the IF function tests if a pupil's mark is more than or equal to 50. If it is then the word 'Passed' appears in the target cell. If the mark is 49 or below, the word 'Failed' appears.

This is the formula for cell B3:

=IF(B3>=50, "Passed","Failed")

Notice how you have to put "" around text values.

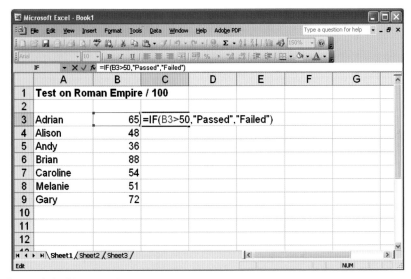

Figure 6.4 **Class results**

If you then click on Enter, the spreadsheet will show who has passed and who has failed (Figure 6.5).

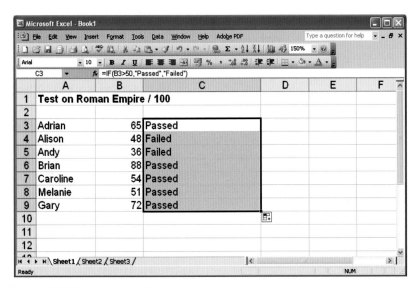

Figure 6.5 **Who has passed?**

AVERAGE

The AVERAGE function calculates the mean of a range of figures.

To find out the average mark obtained in the test results shown in Figure 6.4, the teacher would use the formula:

=AVERAGE(B3:B9)

This would probably be typed into cell B10, as shown in Figure 6.6.

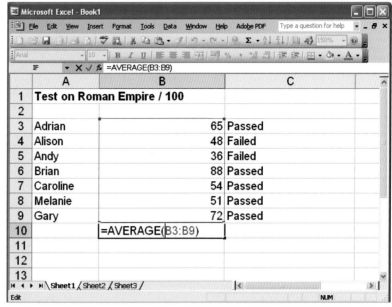

Figure 6.6 What's the average?

Click on Enter to get the result, which is shown in Figure 6.7.

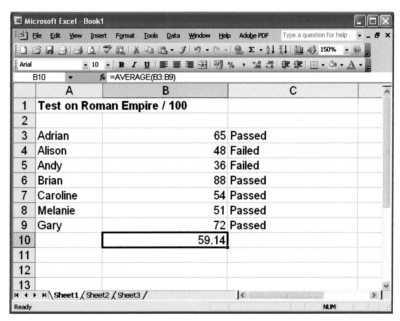

Figure 6.7 It's 59.14 out of 100

Other functions that you might encounter are:

- MAX   finds the biggest number
- MIN   finds the smallest number
- MEDIAN   finds the middle point of a set of numbers
- MODE   finds the most common item in a set of numbers or things.

> Spreadsheet tasks

Now that you know about some common functions, here are some examples of how you can use some of this knowledge. You can find all the files needed on the website at www.hodderplus. co.uk/ocrictfunctionalskills.

Dave is trying to keep track of his money – so that he always knows how much he has spent and how much he has left. Each week he notes down how much money he gets in income and also how much he spends. At the end of each week he adds this information to a spreadsheet. Part of Dave's spreadsheet is shown in Figure 6.8.

	A	B	C	D	E	F
1			**Dave's Money**			
2						
3			**Money in**		**Money spent**	
4	**Date**	**Reason**	**Amount**		**Reason**	**Amount**
5	02/04/2010	Pay	£243.10		Cash	£50.00
6	03/04/2010				Rent	£105.00
7	05/04/2010	Birthday	£50.00		Birthday meal	£46.00
8	06/04/2010				Trousers	£17.00
9	07/04/2010				Trainers	£65.00
10	07/04/2010				Holiday savings	£20.00
11	**End of week**		**£293.10**			**£303.00**
12						
13	09/04/2010	Pay	£294.50		Cash	£75.00
14	10/04/2010				Rent	£105.00
15	11/04/2010				Holiday savings	£20.00
16	12/04/2010				Bus season ticket	£26.00
17	13/04/2010				Kettle	£15.99
18	15/04/2010				Cash	£10.00
19	**End of week**		**£294.50**			**£281.99**

Figure 6.8 Dave's spreadsheet

Dave has set the spreadsheet to add up the money in and the money out each week. He has used the SUM function to do this.

Task 6.1 (Level 1) > > > > >

1 Load Dave's money (Dave's money.xls) using an appropriate application.
2 During the week 12/5/10–19/5/10, Dave received £243.10 and he spent £60 cash on 12/5/10, as well as his normal amount on rent and holiday savings. He also bought a DVD for £11.99 on 18th May. Add this information to Dave's spreadsheet.
3 Insert formulas to work out the total money in and money out, for this week.
4 Dave would like to be able to see how much his income differs from his outgoings each week. Using appropriate formulas and labels, add these to the spreadsheet.
5 Save your work using a filename that will enable Dave to find the modified spreadsheet.
6 Print out the spreadsheet.
7 Print out the spreadsheet showing the formulas.

Dave has provided the following file for you to use:

● Dave's money.xls

Evidence required

● A printout of the completed spreadsheet.
● A printout of the spreadsheet showing formulas.
● A screen dump of the modified file showing where it is stored.

Task 6.2 (Level 1) > > > > >

Louise helps to run a second-hand uniform shop at the local school. She keeps a record of all the items that are for sale in a spreadsheet. Louise has asked for help with her spreadsheet.

The spreadsheet Louise uses is called Second-hand uniforms.

1 Find the following for Louise:
  a the total of all the items for sale
  b the total number of items for sale
  c the total of all the money taken for goods that have been purchased.
2 Louise would like to know the total profit made – this can be calculated by subtracting the total buying price from the total selling price.
3 Louise would also like to know the total number of items sold. Use an appropriate function to show this on the spreadsheet.
4 Print out the final spreadsheet on A4, and then again showing the formulas.

Louise has provided the following file for you to use:

● Second-hand uniforms data

Evidence required

● A printout of the completed spreadsheet.
● A printout of the spreadsheet showing formulas.
● A screen dump of the modified file and where it is stored.

Task 6.3 (Level 2) (examination type task) > > > > >

Louise has been asked for some information about the second-hand uniform shop by the parents association (PTA). The chairman of the PTA has written a letter to Louise – it is shown in Figure 6.9.

Heartswell Secondary School PTA

9a Great Flats
Lower Lane
Heartswell

Mrs. L. Pease
Second-hand Uniform Shop
Heartswell Secondary School
Main Road
Heartswell

10th December 2010

Dear Louise,

Following the meeting of the PTA I have been asked if you could provide us with the following information about the sale of second hand uniforms.

• The most common item sold.
• The lowest price paid for any item and its type.
• The highest price paid for any item and its type.
• The total number of items sold in August with their types and the dates they were sold.
• The increase in profit if the selling margin was increased to 30%.

Yours sincerely

J Tinza-Beanz

J. Tinza-Beanz (Ms)
Chair of PTA

Figure 6.9 The PTA letter to Louise

1 Use the second-hand uniforms data to help Louise to answer the questions written in the letter from Ms Tinza-Beanz.
2 Write a letter for Louise to send back to Ms Tinza-Beanz answering the questions.
3 Save the letter so that it can be found by Louise if it needs to be changed.

Evidence required

- A printout of your spreadsheet showing all the answers required by Ms Tinza-Beanz.
- A printout of the spreadsheet showing formulas.
- A printout of the letter ready for Louise to sign.
- A screen dump showing where your files are stored.

Chapter 7
Charts

> Presenting data

Good data presentation skills are important. Poor graphs and tables often lead both readers and writers to draw wrong conclusions from their data.

> Displaying your data

There are some general rules for displaying numerical data:
- simple is always better
- graphs, tables and charts can be used together
- use clear titles and labels
- provide a description of the main points
- don't compare variables with different scales of magnitude.

> Choosing the best graph

Line graphs

Line graphs are used to represent frequency distributions over time – the y-axis represents frequency; the x-axis represents time or different groups. Use different colours or patterned lines to represent different groups.

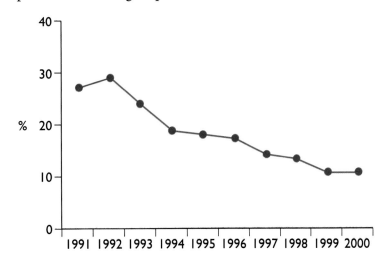

Line graphs can consist of straight lines or curved segments:
- **lines** – use straight lines to connect 'real' data points
- **curves** – use these to represent functional relations between data points or to interpolate data.

Use a line graph:
- to display long data rows
- to forecast data values
- to compare different graphs
- to find and compare changes over time
- to recognise correlation and variation between values
- if the x-axis requires an interval scale
- to display interactions over two levels on the x-axis
- when it defines meaningful patterns (e.g. a zigzag line).

Do not use a line graph:
- if the x-axis has non-numeric values.

Bar charts

Use bar charts to:
- present small data sets over a nominal (e.g. countries, testing conditions) or interval scale (e.g. time)
- compare data.

Do not use bar charts for:
- comparisons – it is better to use one-dimensional scattergraphs, because these are not dominated by bars or columns
- larger data sets – use line charts instead.

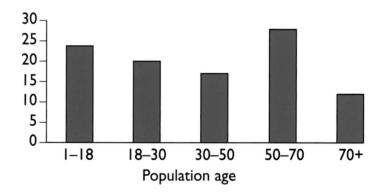

- Always try to arrange the groups that define the bars in a natural order – for example, age.
- If a natural order does not exist, define categories by name.
- Position the bars vertically or horizontally.
- Always make the bars the same width.
- The length of a bar should be proportional to the frequency of the event.

Clustered bar charts

Clustered bar charts are a level 2 skill. In these, bars are presented as clusters of subgroups. These are useful for comparing values across categories. They are sometimes called stacked bar charts.

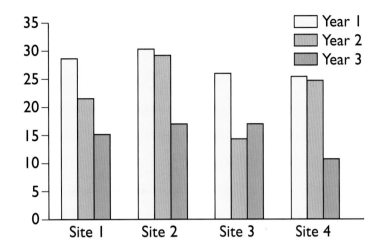

Pie charts

This is a circular (360°) graphic representation of data. It compares subgroups or groups to the whole group or category using differently coloured or patterned segments.

Segments may be pulled out of the pie for emphasis (an 'exploded' pie chart).

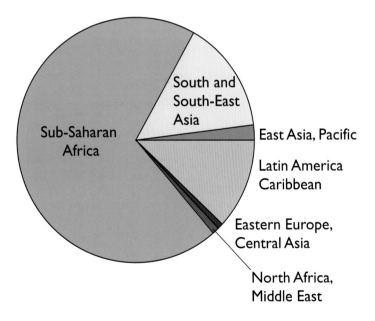

Use pie charts to:

- convey approximate proportional relationships (relative amounts) at a point in time
- compare part of a whole at a given point in time
- emphasise a small proportion of data.

Do not use pie charts:

- for exact comparisons of values, because estimating angles is difficult
- to rank data – use column/bar charts in this case; use multiple column/bar charts for grouped data
- if proportions vary greatly.

Do not use multiple pie charts to compare corresponding parts.

Always exercise care in the use of pie charts.

- Pie charts cannot represent values beyond 100%.
- Each pie chart is valid for one point in time only.
- Pie charts are only suited to presenting percentage values.
- People find it harder to estimate angles than distances.

> How to create graphs

This example is using Microsoft Excel 2003. You should explore similar graph wizards in the spreadsheet you are using. To create a graph, first select the range of data you want to represent. Select only the figures, not the names of the countries or the years or the totals. Then press the Graphs button in the toolbar (Figure 7.1).

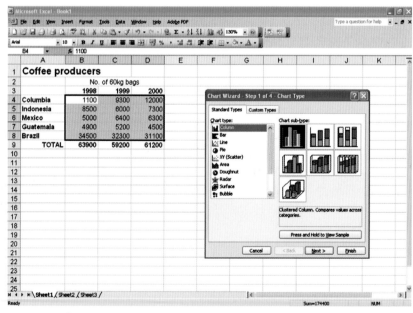

Figure 7.1 **Creating a graph**

A window will pop up with a number of different graphs to choose from. If you click on the Chart Type menu, you'll be able to see what each looks like. The most commonly used ones are the Bar graph, the Line graph and the Pie chart. You can see what your graph will look like if you press on the 'Press and hold to view sample' button.

Once you've chosen your graph, you can go through the Chart Wizard to name the bars in each series – in Figure 7.2 this has been done for 1998, 1999 and 2000. You should also give the graph a title, and name the x- and y-axes.

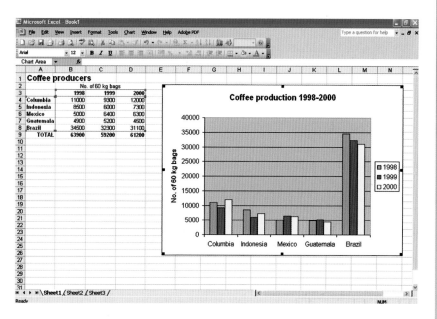

Figure 7.2 **Labelling the graph**

Any graph can be copied and pasted into a word-processing document, a presentation or a graphics application.

> Legends, titles and labels

Every chart should be given a title that describes what it represents, such as 'Sale of chickens in November'.

If a bar chart or pie chart is being displayed then there is usually a legend. The legend is placed near the chart to describe what is represented in it. Some chart wizards will include a legend even when it is not necessary. In those cases make sure the legend is removed.

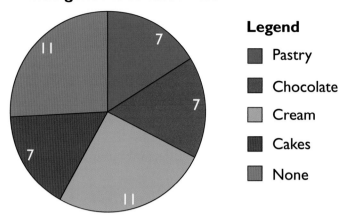

Indulgence food favourites

Legend
- ■ Pastry
- ■ Chocolate
- ■ Cream
- ■ Cakes
- ■ None

Make sure axes are labelled and titled.

Make sure segments of pie charts are clearly labelled or a sensible legend is provided. Sometimes both are needed as in the diagram above.

> Printing charts

When you produce a chart it is almost certainly on the same screen as the data associated with it. If the chart is going to be used away from the spreadsheet, for instance for inserting into a newsletter, you may want to copy it separately from the data. If it was to be placed into a company report you might want to copy some data as well. Planning what data to use and what is not important is a useful skill to develop.

> Chart tasks

Now that you know about using graphs and charts, here are some examples of how you can use some of this knowledge. You can find all the files needed on the website at www.hodderplus.co.uk/ ocrictfunctionalskills.

Task 7.1 (Level 1) > > > > >

Hayley runs the Game, Set and Match table tennis club. She hires the local school hall on Friday evenings, where she often has as many as 50 people of all ages playing matches and training.

Hayley keeps a record of the total income each month in a spreadsheet. She wants to put a chart showing the income from the different types of lessons in September into the October newsletter.

	A	B	C	D
1	Game Set and Match Club			
2				
3	Income Sheet: September 2010			
4			September	
5	Type of income	Item		
6	Lesson	Under 12 boys	£230.00	
7	Lesson	Under 12 girls	£110.00	
8	Lesson	Under 16 boys	£250.00	
9	Lesson	Under 16 girls	£170.00	
10	Lesson	Adult male	£135.00	
11	Lesson	Adult female	£95.00	
12	Sponsorship	Ed's Chips Ltd	£150.00	
13	Sales	Bat	£49.99	
14		Ball (set of 6)	£35.78	
15		Net	£20.00	
16		Club badge	£17.84	
17		T-shirt	£24.00	
18	Match entry fees	Under 16	£200.00	
19	Match entry fees	Adult	£210.00	
20				

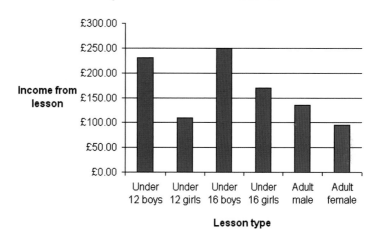

Figure 7.3 Hayley's spreadsheet and chart

1 Produce a chart similar to Hayley's.
2 Insert the chart into the newsletter in an appropriate place.

Hayley has provided these files:

- Club September income data
- October newsletter

Evidence required

- A printout of the October letter with chart.
- Evidence that the altered spreadsheet and newsletters have been saved.

Task 7.2 (Level 1) > > > > >

Matt runs a keep-fit centre. He is interested in the eating habits of the people who come to keep fit. He has given them a questionnaire and has asked them to fill it in.

In one question he asked them to let him know their favourite 'indulgence' food. He would like to produce a pie chart showing the breakdown of the indulgence food preferences.

Part of the questionnaire is shown below:

Question 4

Please tick **one** box to describe your favourite 'indulgence' food.

Chocolate	
Cakes	
Cream/cream pies/meringue	
Pastry/quiche	
Have no indulgence	

Matt has started a spreadsheet containing the answers to many questions. He still has four returned questionnaires to do and he has asked you to fill in the missing details of those he has not yet entered – and then to produce the pie chart for him.

Matt has provided these files:

- Analysis of questionnaire data
- Missing questionnaires

Evidence required

- A printout of the spreadsheet with missing data included.
- A printout of the pie chart, showing the breakdown of the indulgence food preferences.

Task 7.3 (Level 2) > > > > >

Matt is surveying a group of people who attend the local keep-fit centre because he wants to see if there is any relationship between their height and their weight. He also wants two lists:

- a list of weights of all those members who are female and over 1.65 cm tall
- a list of the weights of all males who have an indulgence for chocolate

1 Produce an appropriate chart to show the relationships between height and weight for the members of the keep-fit club.
2 Print the chart.
3 Produce the two lists that Matt requires and print them out.

Matt has provided one file:

- Analysis of questionnaire data

Evidence required

- A printout of the chart.
- A printout of a list of weights of all those members who are female and over 1.65 cm tall.
- A printout of a list of the weights of all males who have an indulgence for chocolate.

Task 7.4 (Level 1) (examination type task) > > > > >

Hasan owns a cafe. He sells a large number of pasties each week. Hasan needs a chart for a report he is writing about the type of pasties sold in the cafe.

1 Produce a bar chart to show the number of each type of pasty sold in February.
2 Make sure the information in the chart is displayed clearly.

Hasan has provided you with the pasty type sales data.

Evidence required

- A printout of the chart.

(A level 2 examination type task would be similar but item 1 would read:

1 Produce a chart to show the number of each type of pasty sold in February.)

> Question for thought

Matt has used a spreadsheet to record the results of the questionnaire and also to produce the lists. A database might be better for Matt to use if he wanted to search the data and produce a number of lists.

Copy the table below and put a tick in the appropriate cells to show what spreadsheets and databases are good at doing.

Task	Spreadsheet	Database
Working out calculations		
Searching and making lists		
Producing charts		
Producing reports		

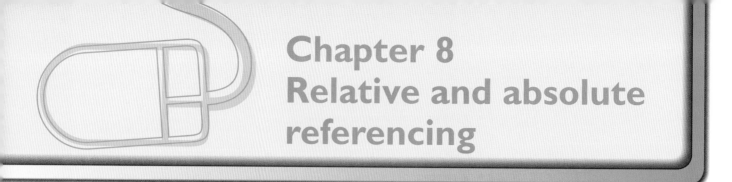

Please note: this chapter is aimed at level 2 students. Absolute referencing is not required at level 1.

Spreadsheets use relative and absolute referencing in formulas. They are important because they ensure that formulas function correctly if you have to change the data.

An example would be a company giving its employees commission. 'Commission' is a reward paid to sales staff – the more they sell, the bigger their commission payment. The rate of commission might change according to the time of year or how well the company is doing. Using absolute referencing, you change the value in just one cell (the rate of commission) and this allows the income calculations based on it to change too.

> Relative cell references

	A	B	C	D	E
1	Egg Sales Commission Q1				
2		Jan Sales £	Feb Sales £	Mar Sales £	
3	George	2600	3620	3830	
4	Mary	4230	4110	4360	
5	Debbie	1500	2580	3400	
6	Amina	5430	5320	5500	
7	Fred	6800	5920	6350	
8	Total	=SUM(B3:B7)			
9					

Figure 8.1 Using the SUM function

As you can see from Figure 8.1, the SUM function is used across cell references B3:B7 to obtain the total sales for January.

If you copy this formula across row 8, it will adjust itself in C8 and D8 using the formulas =SUM(C3:C7) and =SUM(D3:D8) respectively. The cell references change because they are relative, i.e. not fixed.

	A	B	C	D	E
1	Egg Sales Commission Q1				
2		Jan Sales £	Feb Sales £	Mar Sales £	
3	George	2600	3620	3830	
4	Mary	4230	4110	4360	
5	Debbie	1500	2580	3400	
6	Amina	5430	5320	5500	
7	Fred	6800	5920	6350	
8	Total	20560	21550	23440	
9					
10					

Figure 8.2 **Copying the SUM function with relative references**

The total sales for each month are calculated by copying the original formula across the row, which adjusts itself to each month's column as shown in Figure 8.2.

If commission payment is a feature of the rewards paid to sales staff, we need to use absolute cell references.

> Absolute cell references

In Figure 8.3, a total sales column has been added for the sales staff, and it is this column that will be used to calculate the individual commissions earned.

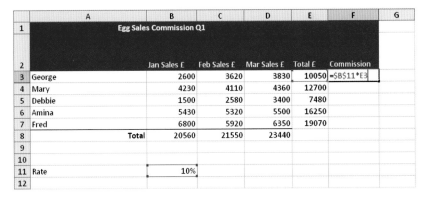

	A	B	C	D	E	F	G
1	Egg Sales Commission Q1						
2		Jan Sales £	Feb Sales £	Mar Sales £	Total £	Commission	
3	George	2600	3620	3830	10050	=$B$11*E3	
4	Mary	4230	4110	4360	12700		
5	Debbie	1500	2580	3400	7480		
6	Amina	5430	5320	5500	16250		
7	Fred	6800	5920	6350	19070		
8	Total	20560	21550	23440			
9							
10							
11	Rate	10%					
12							

Figure 8.3 **Individual sales**

The rate of commission is in cell B11 – it is an absolute reference. You can see in F3 that the formula for calculating the commission rate is

=$B$11*E3

You make a cell absolute using the '$' sign. You can either type it in as '=$B$11' or you can type '=B11' and then press function key F4. Figure 8.4 shows what the table looks like with all the calculations entered. Each member of staff has been rewarded with the correct amount of commission.

	A	B	C	D	E	F	G
1		Egg Sales Commission Q1					
2		Jan Sales £	Feb Sales £	Mar Sales £	Total £	Commission	
3	George	2600	3620	3830	10050	1005	
4	Mary	4230	4110	4360	12700	1270	
5	Debbie	1500	2580	3400	7480	748	
6	Amina	5430	5320	5500	16250	1625	
7	Fred	6800	5920	6350	19070	1907	
8	Total	20560	21550	23440			
9							
10							
11	Rate	10%					
12							

Figure 8.4 Individual sales

Figure 8.5 shows what the table would look like if an absolute reference was not used.

	A	B	C	D	E	F	G
1		Egg Sales Commission Q1					
2		Jan Sales £	Feb Sales £	Mar Sales £	Total £	Commission	
3	George	2600	3620	3830	10050	1005	
4	Mary	4230	4110	4360	12700	0	
5	Debbie	1500	2580	3400	7480	0	
6	Amina	5430	5320	5500	16250	0	
7	Fred	6800	5920	6350	19070	0	
8	Total	20560	21550	23440			
9							
10							
11	Rate	10%					
12							
13							

Figure 8.5 Calculating with relative references

No one gets commission except George. If you use the formula =B11*E3 to calculate his commission, and then copy it down column F, the spreadsheet moves everything down one cell, including column B. B12 is the next cell down – this is empty, and 0*12700 = 0.

Using an absolute reference ($) ensures the commission rate does not get adjusted as the formula is copied down a column.

The employees had worked so hard that their chief decided they should all get 20% commission. To calculate the new commission amounts, all he had to do was change B11 to 20% as shown in Figure 8.6 – and the revised commission amounts appear automatically.

	A	B	C	D	E	F	G
1	Egg Sales Commission Q1						
2		Jan Sales £	Feb Sales £	Mar Sales £	Total £	Commission	
3	George	2600	3620	3830	10050	2010	
4	Mary	4230	4110	4360	12700	2540	
5	Debbie	1500	2580	3400	7480	1496	
6	Amina	5430	5320	5500	16250	3250	
7	Fred	6800	5920	6350	19070	3814	
8	Total	20560	21550	23440			
9							
10							
11	Rate	20%					
12							

Figure 8.6 A revised commission rate

> Referencing tasks (Level 2)

Now that you know about using relative and absolute references, here are some examples of how you can use some of this knowledge. You can find all the files needed on the website at www.hodderplus. co.uk/ocrictfunctionalskills.

Task 8.1 (Level 2) > > > > >

Louise helps to run a second-hand uniform shop. It is a policy of the committee running the shop to place a mark-up of 25% on all items that they sell. In other words, they charge 25% more to the customer than they paid for the item in the first place.

Louise uses a spreadsheet to keep a record of all the items they sell in the shop. The raw data is shown in Figure 8.7, and the formulas used in Figure 8.8.

	B	C	D	E	F	G	H
1	Second Hand Uniform Shop						
2						Selling margin	25%
3	Item	Size	Gender	Date in	Date Sold	Buying price	Selling price
4	School jacket	Small	Female	11/08/2010	25/08/2010	£5.00	£6.25
5	School shirt (white)	Small	Female	18/05/2010	29/07/2010	£5.00	£6.25
6	Track suit top	Medium	Female	09/09/2010	17/06/2010	£1.10	£1.38
7	Track suit bottom	Large	Male	04/03/2010	29/08/2010	£1.42	£1.78
8	School shirt (white)	Small	Male	17/04/2010	24/08/2010	£7.50	£9.38
9	School shirt (white)	Small	Female	29/06/2010	29/10/2010	£7.72	£9.65
10	School jacket	Medium	Male	11/10/2010	14/04/2010	£4.12	£5.15
11	Track suit bottom	Medium	Female	19/06/2010	18/05/2010	£8.31	£10.39
12							

Figure 8.7 Louise's spreadsheet

	A	B	C	D	E	F	G	H
1		Second Hand Uniform Shop						
2							Selling margin	0.25
3	Ref	Item	Size	Gender	Date in	Date Sold	Buying price	Selling price
4	2760	School jacket	Small	Female	40401	40415	5	=$H$2*G4+G4
5	1937	School shirt (white)	Small	Female	40316	40388	5	=$H$2*G5+G5
6	4975	Track suit top	Medium	Female	40430	40346	1.1	=$H$2*G6+G6
7	2738	Track suit bottom	Large	Male	40241	40419	1.42	=$H$2*G7+G7
8	3419	School shirt (white)	Small	Male	40285	40414	7.5	=$H$2*G8+G8
9	1344	School shirt (white)	Small	Female	40358	40480	7.72	=$H$2*G9+G9
10	1841	School jacket	Medium	Male	40462	40282	4.12	=$H$2*G10+G10
11	2975	Track suit bottom	Medium	Female	40348	40316	8.31	=$H$2*G11+G11
12								

Figure 8.8 **The formulas used**

Notice how absolute referencing has been used in cells H4 to H11. If Louise wanted to raise or lower the mark-up she only needs to change the value in one cell. Which cell would Louise have to change to make the mark-up 30%?

1 Using the spreadsheet file that Louise has provided, add appropriate formulas and labels to give the selling price of all items with a mark-up of 30%.
2 Save the file using a sensible filename so that Louise can find it.
3 Print a copy of the spreadsheet.

Louise has provided one file:

- Second-hand shop mark-up data.xls

Evidence required

- A printout of the spreadsheet showing selling prices.
- A printout of the spreadsheet showing the formulas.
- A screen dump showing the file saved using a meaningful name.

Task 8.2 (Level 2) > > > > >

Claudia Bissell runs a Christmas club. The idea is that each member collects money for the next Christmas holiday, and at the same time they donate a small proportion to a charity. They collect the money over a period of 12 months.

Each year, the club members decide which charity to support and what proportion of their savings will go to the charity. This year they decide to contribute 5%.

Claudia has decided to use ICT to help in recording the data and in working out various figures. She has decided to use a spreadsheet and has planned a layout – but she needs help with the formulas.

Claudia wants to know:

- what contribution each member will make to charity
- the total each member needs to save altogether
- how much they must save each month
- what the total amount given to charity will be
- who saves the largest amount
- who saves the smallest amount

Claudia has saved her spreadsheet using the name Christmas club data.xls.

1 Complete the spreadsheet for Claudia.
2 Save it using a filename she can recognise.
3 Print the raw data in the spreadsheet.
4 Print the spreadsheet so that its formulas can be seen.
5 Use your completed spreadsheet to work out what percentage the members would have to contribute to charity to make a contribution of around £1000.

Hint: use trial and error to change the percentage contribution and see how it affects the total.

Evidence required

- A printout of the spreadsheet.
- A printout of the spreadsheet showing the formulas.
- A screen dump showing the file saved using a meaningful name.

Task 8.3 (Level 2) (examination type task) > > > > >

Greta sells boxes of mixed seasonal vegetables. Each box costs £4.50.

Greta needs to know the total number of boxes sold from week 1 to week 40. She also needs to know the total income each week and the total income for all 40 weeks.

Greta has provided you with the vegetable box sales data.

1 Find the information Greta needs.

Evidence required

- A printout of the information Greta requires.
- A printout showing formulas used.

Greta wants to know how much more income she would have received if each box had cost £4.99.

2 Find the information Greta needs.

Evidence required

- A printout of the information Greta requires.
- A printout showing formulas used.
- A screen dump showing where you stored the file for Greta.

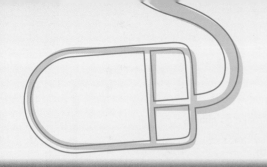

Chapter 9
Diagrams and logos

Logos appear on almost all printed and electronic materials. They are the most prominent identity item for many businesses – they represent instant brand recognition. Logos are important because customers remember them, even subconsciously, and this affects what they buy. Logos can have positive or negative associations but the best will not pass unnoticed. Logos are part of company identity – and being noticed in a competitive world is vital. Logo designs should not be complicated – they usually work best when they are kept simple.

Please note: designing a logo is not part of the functional skills standards and will not be examined, but the skills of manipulating graphics can be practised using the activities in this chapter.

> Think about the audience

Who is your likely audience? Make your logo relevant to how they see the world. A company specialising in package holidays for the over 65s will not have the same audience as a high-end niche manufacturer of smart phones.

Your logo should entertain and engage the audience – not be so obscure that the message (and potential business) is lost, but not be so literal that it spells out the company's name. It should, however, relate to the business in some shape or form as a prompt to memory.

A good logo	A bad logo
Looks professional.	Looks amateurish.
Is simple.	Is complex and hard to understand.
Will be useful over the lifetime of the company.	Is fashionable.
Is also effective in black and white.	Needs colour to work.
Has very few fonts.	Uses too many fonts.

> Designing logos

Remember that the design of logos will not be examined, this is just for fun. You will need to know how to manipulate logos and decide where to place them.

The basic simple shapes of circles, squares and triangles can be very effective in logo design.

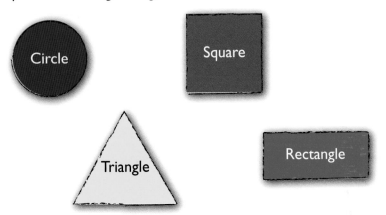

Before designing a logo, you need to think about the image you want to show. For example, a transport company might want to show swift delivery and as a result produce a logo that includes arrows or that shows movement.

Image

Before you start, think about what the logo is trying to express and what type of company it will represent. The image could be:

- **bold** – is it trustworthy? dependable? experienced? Such logos might have lots of straight lines, bold forms, solid objects and squares.
- **high-tech** – is it modern? fast-moving? technologically advanced? Such logos might have triangular forms that represent conflict, tension and action.
- **flair** – is it customer-oriented? creative? responsive? Such logos might have soft movement through wavy lines, or circular forms that are protective and infinite.

Graphics

Ideally, logos should be created in a drawing program – illustration or drawing software produces vector graphic artwork. These are ideal because they are scalable.

Word-processing software, such as Microsoft Word, and presentation software, such as PowerPoint, are not intended to act as logo-design software but they are often used to create simple logos. The main toolbar is a great place to start. There you'll find simple shapes, lines, colours and styles.

Shapes such as these have certain subconscious meanings:
- the circle is protective or infinite
- the square denotes stability, equality and honesty
- the triangle suggests tension, movement conflict or action.

You can use shapes together, with colour as shown in Figure 9.1.

Figure 9.1 **Using Word's drawing tools**

It's a good idea to link individual shapes so they all move together. You can do this by holding the Shift key down, then clicking on each shape in turn, then right-clicking and selecting Grouping/ Group.

You can build composite shapes, such as that shown in Figure 9.2, by copying and pasting. Here the initial triangle has been copied twice. To do this, click on the original shape and press Ctrl-C. Copy twice by pressing Ctrl-V twice.

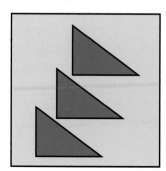

Figure 9.2 **Using copy and paste**

You can use some of the 3-D features; you can stretch and tilt shapes; add texture and shading – the possibilities are wide indeed (Figure 9.3).

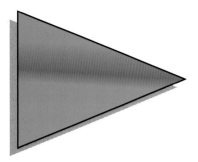

Figure 9.3 **Many possibilities**

Clipart offers yet more possibilities. These can also be useful when creating logos – Figure 9.4 shows three cog clipart images grouped in a coloured circular background; Figure 9.5 is made by using a clipart car, tilted upwards to give the impression of haste.

Figure 9.4 **Using clipart**   Figure 9.5 **A clipart car**

If the chosen image doesn't suit as a whole, you can crop the bits you don't want out. An example is given in Figure 9.6.

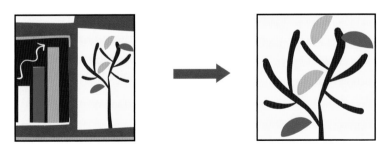

Figure 9.6 **Cropping an image**

Figure 9.7 shows the effect of rotating an image about a point.

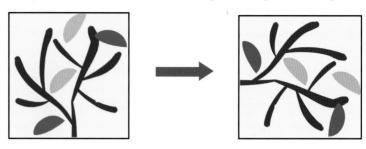

Figure 9.7 Rotating an image

You can change the colours in the image (Figure 9.8), make it smaller by dragging a corner point inwards, stretch it by dragging the middle point outwards …

Figure 9.8 Endless possibilities

As always, the best way to learn about software is to use it. Play around with the different functions and buttons to create your own logos and graphics.

> Diagrams and logos tasks

Now that you know about using logos, here are some examples of how you can use some of this knowledge. You can find all the files needed on the website at www.hodderplus.co.uk/ocrictfunctionalskills.

Task 9.1 (Level 1) > > > > >

George Bunting is the editor of the Chestpury Local History Society newsletter. The newsletter is produced every month. George wants a logo to appear on the banner at the top of the newsletter. At the moment it looks like this:

Chestpury Local History Society
Newsletter No. 25 March
Editor George Bunting Contact email g.bunting@cbury.coz

George has asked Chantelle Vernon, who is studying GCSE ICT, to create two examples for the committee to look at. Chantelle has produced the two logos shown in Figure 9.9.

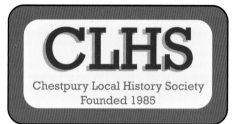

(a)

Chestpury Local History Society

Founded 1985

(b)

Figure 9.9 (a) Logo 1 and (b) Logo 2

1 Decide which logo you would choose if you were George. Write down two reasons for your choice of logo.
2 Produce Logo 1 and save it.
3 Produce Logo 2 using the old ruin picture and save it.

George has provided the file:

- Ruin image

Evidence required

- Two reasons for choosing a particular logo.
- A printout of the two logos.
- A screen dump showing where the logos are stored.

Task 9.2 (Level 1) > > > > >

You have been asked by a local club called 'Keep Fit Fun Runners' to produce a logo. The club has abbreviated their name to KFFR. They would like the logo to use on their documents and on the runner's vests.

1 Produce a suitable logo for the KFFR. Re-read the part of the chapter about using logos to represent speed or movement – this might help your choice of design.
2 Print a copy of the logo.

Evidence required

- A printout of your logo for KFFR.
- A screen dump showing where the logo is stored.

Susan works in Chestpury Infant School. She likes to read Beatrix Potter books to the children because they love the characters. She wants to send a reading list to the children's parents each term and she thought that a logo on the leaflet to be sent home would be appropriate if it had a Beatrix Potter theme.

She thinks that the leaflet should have a structure like that shown in Figure 9.10.

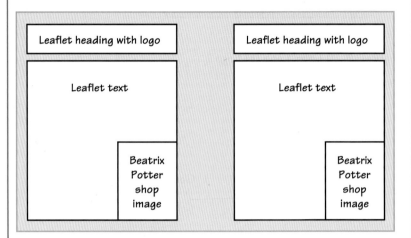

Figure 9.10 Susan's leaflet structure

Susan visited the Beatrix Potter shop in Gloucester and took some pictures. Use these to help you to create a logo for the handout. Susan has also provided you with the text she wants included in the leaflet.

1 Create a logo for the leaflet.
2 Create a suitable heading for the leaflet and incorporate the logo.
3 Complete the leaflet using the text Susan has provided. Orientate the page to landscape and arrange for two leaflets to be printed on a single A4 page.

Susan has provided the files:

- Beatrix Potter shop image
- Beatrix Potter old shop image
- Reading with your children text

Evidence required

- A printout of your logo.
- A printout of the leaflet.
- A screen dump showing where the leaflet and logo are stored.

Task 9.4 (Level 1) > > > > >

In Chapter 3 on newsletters, you were told about Sheila and the geocachers. She would like a logo for her newsletter – Figure 9.11 shows her first effort. Can you improve on it for her?

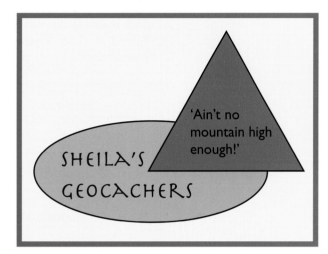

Figure 9.11 Sheila's logo

1 Create a suitable logo for the geocachers newsletter. Remember that they like to hike, explore, climb mountains and so on. You can use the internet to search for suitable clipart or images if you want.
2 Print out your improved logo for Sheila.

Susan has provided the files:

• Geocache logo image

Evidence required

• A printout of the logo.
• A screen dump showing where the logo is stored.

The annual general meeting of the Keep Fit Fun Runners is to take place on November 25th beginning at 7.30 p.m. There were problems with the seating last year.

George Riley, the KFFR secretary, needs a single-sheet seating plan to go in the envelope with the invitation to the AGM. His sketch is shown in Figure 9.12 – the logo you produced in Task 9.2 should be included in an appropriate place.

> Heading
>
> Committee
>
> Treasurer Chairman Secretary
> Stage
>
> Members and guests

Figure 9.12 Rough seating plan

1 Produce the seating plan for George.

Evidence required

- A printout of the seating plan leaflet on one side of A4 paper.
- A screen dump showing where the leaflet is stored.

Chapter 10
Databases

Databases are used to collect, store and manipulate data. You may need to work with databases on a regular basis to integrate stored data or add customers or other information required. The data in a database is held in tables. Each table is made up of rows (records) and columns (fields).

There are many different reasons why you would use a database – the accuracy of the data and correct manipulation are most important for the right results.

Databases range from being very simple to very complex. There are two main types of database programs. At the simple end there are 'flat-file' databases – also called single-file or list managers. At the other end are 'relational' databases – with these you can create a range of databases that are linked to each other. Small businesses and large organisations use these.

The main operations on data involve the adding, editing, deleting and searching of information and this is what we concentrate on in this chapter.

> Field names and data types

Data is in many types. Some of the usual types of data are text, number, currency or dates. When recording data in both spreadsheets and databases you have to decide what type of data is being recorded so that the software can deal with it appropriately and present it properly. The cells containing that data have to be formatted using the software. Some data types are shown below.

Data type	Example	Description
Number (integer)	17	An **integer** is a whole number (positive or negative but no fractions).
Number (real)	23.67	A **real** number is any number including whole numbers and fractions. The software you are using will let you decide how many decimal places to use.
Text or string	John Smith	Generally letters but could also contain numbers and punctuation.
Date/Time	04/10/06 12:23:09	Any time or date. The way the time or date is displayed depends on how it is formatted.
Currency	£12.50	Money
Boolean	Yes	The data can have only two possible opposing states such as yes or no, true or false, male or female.

Field names must be chosen with care. They should be descriptive and brief as they will be at the top of a column and if you make the field name too long then the table becomes awkward to use. There are many examples of field names in this book and in the tasks you are asked to complete.

> Adding data to a database

When you add data to an existing database, it is important to follow the existing format and to enter the new details into the correct fields. This ensures consistency across your data, which is really important – it will also make it easier to view and change the data if needed later.

Good database practice	Bad database practice
Putting the data in the correct fields.	Data entered in wrong fields.
Entering accurate data.	Misspelling of data.
Have as much data as possible to enter.	Missing data fields.

Some databases will not allow you to save the information you have entered unless you have filled in all the required fields – this is to help with accuracy and consistency across the whole of the database.

Adding data is generally as easy as opening a table or a new record, filling in the blank fields then clicking 'Save' or 'Next' to save your data.

> Online databases

There are thousands of databases on the internet that are available for consultation. Which one you use will depend on what you are searching for.

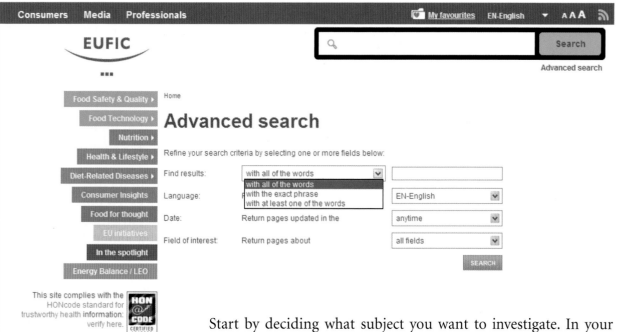

Start by deciding what subject you want to investigate. In your search engine, enter a suitable keyword – for example:

database music

You'll get lots of hits on databases on music.
If you type

database cars

you'll see thousands of hits on databases on cars. You'll be amazed at the number of databases out there for you to consult.

> How to search

Once you've found the right database, either online or one you have been given or created, you then have to consult the mass of data it contains. First of all, decide what information you are searching for – all databases have their own search engine and they all work in a similar way.

Although all databases are different, most of them usually require you to do a search before you can access the data. You will need to be able to search through data for many different kinds of information:

- perhaps you want to find someone you have completed work for in the past and need to check the price you charged
- maybe you have been asked to search for data entered in a specific period.

A search can be done in a variety of ways – depending on the available search fields. Each record usually has a unique identifier – a reference or account number – and this can be used in a 'simple' search. However, if you don't know the reference then you may need to do a more in-depth or advanced search using multiple fields; this option helps to narrow down your search.

The most common online database search uses a box in which you enter your keywords and click on 'Search'. However, if you want to search for something specific, you might need to do a complex search using Boolean operators.

Search forms

Some online databases have a search form to fill in. For example, the database on funfair rides worldwide has an advanced search form as shown in Figure 10.1.

You fill in the boxes and click 'Search' for the result. For a maximum number of potential hits, fill in as few boxes as possible. The search shown in Figure 10.1 was too restricted and there were no hits. However, if you just want to know about rides operating in the UK, you get 413 hits.

Simple search

With a unique identifier you can usually enter this in a single search field, which takes you directly to the record you are looking for.

The main search screen usually appears when you open the application and you have to enter some search criteria before you can access anything within the application. Once in your main search screen, you can enter the unique identifier into the relevant search field, and then clicking 'Search' will bring up the matching record.

Complex search

A complex search works on the same principle as a simple search. If you don't know the reference, you can use a variety of other criteria such as postcode, surname, etc.

Most databases include the option to be able to search using a small amount of information. For example, if you are looking for somebody who lives in your area then you can enter the first part of the postcode. This will bring up a list of records that match this and you can then probably find the record you need from the list.

To narrow down a search you can use more than one field. For example, if you know that a Mr Taylor lives in the area of OX16 you can enter these into the relevant search fields. This produces a list of all people with surname 'Taylor' who live in the 'OX16' area.

Some search options also give you the option of choosing whether you want to search the whole field or just part of it and whether it should be an exact match and so on.

Boolean search

Boolean searches use commands – or 'operators' – to limit the number of potential hits and increase the likelihood that those hits

Figure 10.1 **Advanced search form**

are useful. The most commonly used operators are AND, OR and NOT. They are case-sensitive, so always write them in capital letters.

- **AND** will give you hits on both/all words – e.g. enter 'act II AND traviata' in the search box in the Aria database (www.aria-database.com) and you will get 3 matches concerning Act II of the opera La Traviata.
- **OR** will result in hits containing either word, it doesn't matter which – e.g. 'act II OR traviata' gives about 645 hits that match either 'act II' or 'traviata'.
- **NOT** searches for documents that have the first word/phrase but not the second word – e.g. 'heart attack uk NOT london'. If you use this search in the PubMed database, the section on clinical trials, the database will be searched for heart attacks in the UK but excluding London, generating a total of about 26 hits.

Alternative NOT operators are BUT NOT and AND NOT, or putting a minus sign before the phrase or word to be ignored – e.g. 'heart attack uk –london'.

> Searching using logical operators

You can search a database in many ways. One way of searching is to use **logical operators**. These use the signs:
- = meaning 'equal to'
- > meaning 'greater than'
- < meaning 'less than'
- <> meaning 'not equal to'
- <= meaning 'less than or equal to'
- >= meaning 'greater than or equal to'

The last two operators are required only at level 2.

Member	Title	First name	Surname	Category	Gender	Attendance
325	Mr	John	Jones	Full adult	Male	27
326	Mrs	Julie	Hunter	Life	Female	12
327	Mr	Nai	Tegap	Associate adult	Male	25
328	Mr	Steve	Olden	Full adult	Male	27
329	Mr	Jimmy	Pelling	Full adult	Male	23
330	Miss	Ruth	Quinton	Full child	Female	4
331	Mrs	Geraldine	Palmer	Associate adult	Female	21
332	Miss	Carole	Read	Full child	Female	7
333	Mrs	Jodie	Williams	Full adult	Female	18
334	Ms	Andrea	Baldwin	Life	Female	17

Using the section of the database above we could search for all the males. We would use a simple search with the = operator.

Gender = Male

This would produce the following records.

325	Mr	John	Jones	Full adult	Male	27
327	Mr	Nai	Tegap	Associate adult	Male	25
328	Mr	Steve	Olden	Full adult	Male	27
329	Mr	Jimmy	Pelling	Full adult	Male	23

Gender <> Male would produce a list of all the female members.

To find those who had attended fewer than 12 meetings we could use

Attendance <12

This would produce the following records.

| 330 | Miss | Ruth | Quinton | Full child | Female | 4 |
| 332 | Miss | Carole | Read | Full child | Female | 7 |

> Editing data

There are many reasons why you may need to edit data – for example, updating an address or correcting a mistype. Editing is a really valuable tool in databases but should be used with caution because you don't want to remove something of high importance from a field.

Some fields may be locked to prevent editing unless you click a specific button to unlock the fields – this edit button usually is shown next to the corresponding fields. On saving your changes, the fields will be locked again.

> Deleting data

All databases have the option of deleting data or records should you need to:

- perhaps you entered some information incorrectly and need to delete what you had saved
- you may have out-of-date data that you no longer need.

Most databases have the option to delete multiple lines of data, or they may let you delete just certain fields. Again it is important that you use this option carefully because once your data has been deleted in most cases it is difficult to retrieve it.

When deleting data within a record, you can select the 'Edit' option as described above.

To delete selected records you will need to go through the same search options as described above and there will be a 'Delete' option on the results screen.

> Filtering databases

Flat-file databases can be set up using sophisticated programs such as Microsoft Access – but it is possible to use a spreadsheet program such as Microsoft Excel as a flat-file database. All the tasks that follow can be carried out with a database or a spreadsheet application.

> Database tasks

Now that you know about using databases, here are some examples of how you can use some of this knowledge. You can find all the files needed on the website at <u>www.hodderplus.co.uk/ocrictfunctionalskills</u>.

Task 10.1 (Level 2) > > > > >

George runs the Chestpury Local History Society. He has a produced a file of members and he wants to write to them all about a special presentation to be made to all the female life-members.

George produced the letter shown in Figure 10.2.

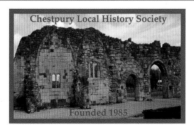

Chestpury Local History Society

George Bunting
The Grange
Chestpury

Contact email g.bunting@cbury.coz

27th July

Dear Member,
We are delighted to announce our annual endeavour awards to this society. This award ceremony will take place in the Village Hall on Saturday September 24th. We welcome you to attend and support our lady life members who have achieved this award.

We are inviting the following members to receive the GBA.

Figure 10.2 Letter from George

1 Produce the list of female life-members for George using an appropriate application.
2 George has provided a letter and he wants you to add the list of female life-members in an appropriate place.
3 Print out the letter.
4 Save your letter using a suitable filename so that George can find the letter later.

George has provided the files:

- Invitation letter
- Chestpury LHS data

Evidence required

- A printout of the list of female life-members.
- A printout of the completed letter.
- A screen dump showing where the letter is stored.

Task 10.2 (Level 2) > > > > >

Produce a list of all the adult members of the Chestpury Local History Society who started their membership before 1st June 2009.

George has provided the file:

- Chestpury LHS data

Evidence required

- A printout of the list of adult members who started before 1/6/09.

Task 10.3 (Level 2) > > > > >

Some new members have joined the Chestpury Local History Society and some have changed their details by changing their membership category or by getting married. One has stopped being a member.

George has asked you to update the database. He has provided a list for you to work from. He needs a copy of the updated membership list on one side of A4 paper.

- Anne Norris has married Barry Green
- New member Lloyd Williams full adult member 2/10/10
- New member Annie Southerly aged 10 joined as full member 3/10/10
- Nick Parke has become a life-member
- Nai Tegap has not paid his membership fees and has moved away – please delete
- Kerry's son Simon is now an adult member

1 Update the database for George.
2 Print out a copy of the updated membership list for George.

George has provided the file:

- Chestpury LHS data

Evidence required

- A printout of the updated membership list.
- Proof that an appropriate application was used.

Task 10.4 (Level 1) (examination type task) > > > > >

George runs a local history society. He needs a list of male members and a list of female members of the society.

1 Produce the lists for George.
2 Make sure the information is displayed clearly.

George has provided you with the Chestpury LHS data.

Evidence required

- A printout of the two lists.

Chapter 11
Database sorting

Once you have established a database, there are many ways you can use it to your advantage. For example, you can sort the data to make it easier to use – you can also produce reports and lists, which enable you to manipulate or view the data on a much larger scale.

Databases are relatively easy to use – once you know the basics. The tools you will learn about in this chapter will be useful when viewing and changing data in your database.

> Sorting data

Sorting data allows you to sort a list of information into a particular order – for example, date order so that you can view the most recent transactions first; or reverse the order and have the oldest transactions first in the list.

Different databases use different methods for doing this but the most common are:

- clicking on the header at the top of the data for the particular field you want to sort by (once for ascending; twice for descending).
- using a 'Sort A/Z' button – click in the field you want to sort and then click the 'Sort A/Z' or 'Sort Z/A' for an ascending sort or a descending sort respectively.
- using a 'Wizard' to pull out certain data from specified fields – perhaps when you are comparing the data.

For a more complex sort, you may have the option to apply a filter – through which you select a particular record, and then click the 'Filter button' to get all similar records (with respect to the field you wish to sort) matched together. You can also impose criteria in the Filter button to filter out the data you want.

> Producing reports or lists

At some point, you will want to view your data in report or list form. All databases have this really valuable option.

Reports

If you wanted to target customers within a certain area, you can produce a report that will give you a list of relevant customers.

All database programs have a Report function that can be used to produce various lists and reports according to specified criteria.

Sometimes there are reports already set up or formatted to allow quick and easy access to the data. You usually also have the option of editing the report depending on the fields of data you require. You generally have an opportunity to view your report in various formats, whether you are exporting into a spreadsheet, creating a text file or printing the data.

Many databases include a Wizard to help you through the process of producing a list or table, but in some you will have to go through the Report function manually.

Whichever you use, you can:

- Select the data you want listed in the report – for example, all customers who required work during the previous 3 months.
- Choose the format of your report – landscape or portrait? field order? etc. If you use a Wizard to produce the report then its layout may need editing.
- Enter a title for your report
- Choose how you would like to view your data – as a spreadsheet or text file? as a PDF? send straight to the printer?
- Save the report in case you need to view the data again, or want to use the report some other time.

Once you have your report printed, you can view the data to make any decisions you need. Whatever reason you needed the report for, this is a really powerful tool for viewing any of the data in your database in any way you want.

Lists

Lists are dealt with in exactly the same way as reports – but you could make them simpler by choosing the particular fields of data you want a list of.

Reports and lists both work with the same thought in mind – to produce clear and concise data from within your database in a form that is easy to read.

> Database sorting tasks

Now that you know about using sorting databases, here are some examples of how you can use some of this knowledge. You can find all the files needed on the website at www.hodderplus.co.uk/ocrictfunctionalskills.

Saqib is a teacher. He is planning a series of lessons about databases and he wants to give a lesson about sorting data. He intends to tell his students about different ways in which lists of data can be presented:

- alphabetical – data is listed in order of the letters of the alphabet
- numerical – data is listed in counting order
- chronological – data is listed in order of time and/or date

In each of the above cases the list can be:

- ascending – data is listed with the smallest value first
- descending – data is listed with the largest value first

Saqib has asked you to help in producing the lesson series. He has prepared some data about camera equipment purchased on EBay (Figure 11.1) and he would like you to sort the data into different lists that he can use in a presentation to show the different ways in which data can be sorted.

Example data			
ID	Item	Date acquired	Amount paid
1	old camera	23/04/2010	£12.45
2	35 mm film	24/04/2010	£0.99
3	camera tripod	03/03/2010	£3.56
4	instruction booklet	15/05/2010	£1.35
5	lens cover	18/03/2010	£2.00
6	flash unit	20/03/2010	£5.23

Figure 11.1 Data supplied by Saqib

He would like the data sorted:

- alphabetically ascending and descending
- numerically ascending and descending
- chronologically ascending and descending

1 Produce the six different lists for Saqib.
2 Create a presentation for Saqib to show the class, using your six lists as illustrations.

Saqib has provided the file:

- Sorting data

Evidence required

- Six lists of sorted data.
- A presentation with at least three slides.
- A screen dump showing where the files are stored.

Task 11.2 (Level 1) > > > > >

Chestpury Local History Society is run by George Bunting. The society organises trips to places of historic interest, and often invites visiting speakers to talk at the monthly meeting.

George keeps the details of the members of the society on a database. He is preparing the annual report and needs to insert a number of lists in his report about the composition of the members of the society.

George needs lists of:

- all the data in descending order of date of joining
- all the data in alphabetical order of member surnames
- all the data in ascending order of membership number

1 Produce the three lists for George.
2 Print the three lists.

George has provided the file:

- Chestpury LHS data

Evidence required

- Three lists of sorted data.
- A presentation with at least three slides.
- A screen dump showing where the files are stored.

Task 11.3 (Level 2) (examination type task) > > > > >

Brenda is a fan of music from the 1960s. She likes to collect old records and has kept the details in a file. She is particularly interested in old records by a group called the Beatles.

Brenda needs:

- A list showing the order in which the records were published
- A list in the alphabetical order of record title
- A list of the number 1 hits in each year with the titles arranged alphabetically within the year

1 Produce the lists for Brenda.
2 Save any files you create so that Brenda can easily find them.

Brenda has provided the following file:

- Beatles records data

Evidence required

- The three lists you have created for Brenda.
- A screen dump showing where the files you have created are stored.

Chapter 12
Examination techniques

However good your ICT skills are, it is easy to miss marks in the Functional Skills examination by simple practical omissions and a failure to present work properly.

Some of the ways you can improve your mark are given below.

> Your name

Every piece of paper produced in the examination must have your name on it, otherwise it will not be given any marks. The best way to do this is to put it in a header or a footer. If you put your name anywhere else it may spoil the work you are trying to present.

- Make sure that you know how to create headers and footers in all the applications you use.
- Make it a practice to put your name in a header or footer of every piece of work you do so that you do it automatically when in an examination situation.

> Use meaningful folder and file names

There are always marks in the examination for producing evidence that you have saved your work sensibly and successfully. The examiners are looking for meaningful file and folder names and your ability to display these properly. There are many pitfalls, so always pay attention to the following.

- When saving a file, use a name that describes what is in the file – not who saved it or when. An example of a good filename is 'Map of Epcot Centre'; an example of a bad filename is 'My Task 4.3 map'.
- When producing a screen dump of files, make sure the names are large enough and clear enough to read – if you can't read them, then neither can the examiner.
- Set the 'View' for the folder to 'List' or 'Detail' – 'Icon' mode will often obscure the full filename.
- Make sure the whole filename is fully shown.

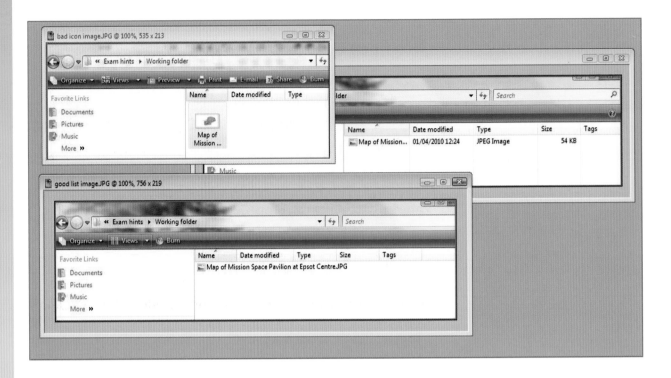

When creating folders you should follow the same advice given above for naming and producing screen dumps. You will need to use folders when you have more than one file and the files are of different topics. For instance if you have created files for letters to Jon and you have created a presentation for Jon you might want to create two folders and call them 'Jon's letters' and 'Jon's presentation'. You can then keep all the files neatly so that they can easily be found when you need them.

> Saving files and pages from the internet

Saving files and pages from the internet should be practised as you will often have to use this skill in the examination. Check with your teacher if you are not sure how to use the internet browser you are working with to save pages and files.

> Spreadsheets

When you are working with spreadsheets, pay attention to the following.
- All columns are sufficiently wide to display all the data.
- All added data is suitably labelled and the labels are:
  accurate
  meaningful
  correctly positioned, so as to be unambiguous.

- Formula printouts show all the formulas – if the complete formula cannot be seen, it cannot be awarded marks.
- If you are sorting data then make sure that all the data is sorted, not just one column – otherwise the data in your spreadsheet will no longer be meaningful.
- Make sure that all the data in a particular column is formatted appropriately and has the same format for every entry. For instance, currency can be shown as £ 7.00 (known as accountancy format) or £7.00 (known as currency format) – make sure you only use one format.

> Graphs and charts

In Chapter 7, you learned which charts to use in different circumstances. However, there are some golden rules that apply to all charts:

- Give a chart a title that describes what is being charted.
- Use an appropriate legend, or remove the legend altogether if it is not useful.
- Make sure that axes are labelled and titled.
- Make sure that segments of pie charts are clearly labelled, or that a sensible legend is given.
- Make sure your chart is readable – many perfectly good coloured screen charts become difficult or impossible to read when printed in black and white.

> Consistency

Any piece of ICT work you present should have consistency. This means that the styles and themes that you use should remain constant. These themes might include:

- fonts
- colours
- formats.

> Tables

When you insert a table you should take care to:

- show all grid lines
- use an appropriate number of rows and columns
- keep font sizes and styles consistent within the table
- keep alignment consistent within rows and columns
- adjust the column widths so that there is not too much white space.

There are a number of things wrong with the presentation of the table below. Can you find them all? Copy the table and format it correctly.

Name	height(cm)	Waight(kg)	Body Mass index (BMI)
John	165	55	20.2
Sue	157.00	50.00	20.30
Matt	173	51.00	17.00
chris	171	56	19.2

You would have to spot and correct at least 12 mistakes before presenting this table for assessment. Can you spot them all? The table should look like this.

Name	Height (cm)	Weight (kg)	Body mass index (BMI)
John	165	55	20.2
Sue	157	50	20.3
Matt	173	51	17.0
Chris	171	56	19.2

> Lists

Lists often have to be produced from spreadsheets and databases. When you are asked to produce a list:
- make sure you give the list a meaningful title
- only list the fields (or columns) relevant to the title
- do not include columns if they are mentioned in the title.

For instance, if you are asked to provide the names of all female cyclists in a club, you would list their names only – not all the redundant data.

Correct list

Female cyclists
Zoe
Bella
Josie
Samantha
Kylie

Incorrect list

Female cyclists		
Zoe	Female	Cyclist
Bella	Female	Cyclist
Josie	Female	Cyclist
Samantha	Female	Cyclist
Kylie	Female	Cyclist

Index